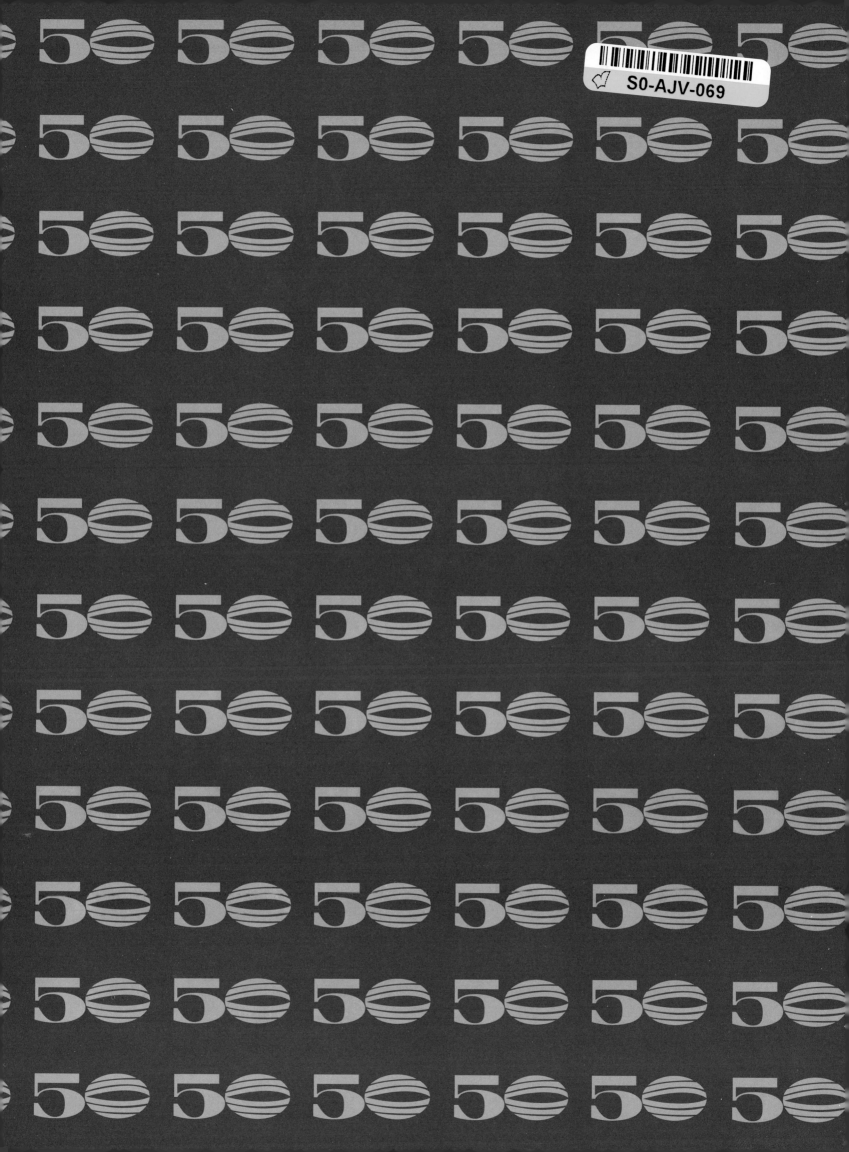

NBAA's Tribute to Business Aviation

By Robert A. Searles
with Robert B. Parke

ISBN 0-9627180-0-9

© 1997 National Business Aviation Association, Inc.
Published in the United States by NBAA at
1200 18th St. NW
Suite #400
Washington, D.C. 20036

First Printing, September 1997

Production Director & Author
Robert A. Searles

Design & Layout
David M. Perry

Collaboration
Robert B. Parke

Printed by Colorcraft of Virginia, Inc.
Sterling, Virginia

© 1997 Mike Vines

TABLE OF CONTENTS

ACKNOWLEDGMENTS

As the author of *Business & Commercial Aviation (B/CA)* magazine's "Reflections" historical column, I am constantly checking my chronologies to see when the next major aviation anniversary will occur.

In late 1995, I noted that the 50th Anniversary of the National Business Aviation Association (NBAA) would be in 1997. So I asked my old boss, John W. "Jack" Olcott, who was Editor and Publisher of *B/CA* before becoming NBAA President, if the Association might be interested in having someone update former NBAA President John H. Winant's landmark book, *Keep Business Flying,* which covered NBAA's first 40 years.

Jack was interested, but he proposed a larger, more ambitious project. He wanted a book that would combine Winant's detailed history of NBAA with a review of the Association's more recent activities. He envisioned an original work that would trace the origins of business flying, which started long before NBAA's predecessor organization, the Corporation Aircraft Owners Association, was formed in 1947. The "coffee-table-style" book was to be oversized and amply illustrated to appeal to aviators and enthusiasts alike. Thus, the final product— *NBAA's Tribute to Business Aviation*—was the brainchild of Jack Olcott.

Along the way, Kathleen Hull, NBAA's Vice President of Conventions & Seminars, provided valuable ideas and input while serving as director of the book project. NBAA Assistant Marketing Manager of Convention & Seminars, Jeff Lund, ably served as an efficient second in command.

A number of NBAA Staff members—past and present—also helped support the project: Cassandra J. Bosco, Cheryl A. Chick, Robert A. Cooke, Ann W. Devers, William M. Fanning, E.H. Moe Haupt, Jonathan Howe, Richard Lampl, Frederick B. McIntosh, Joseph Ponte, Jr., John A. Pope, Martha Schultz, Lisa Paitz Spindler, William H. Stine II, Marcy Tate, Pete West and C. Dennis Wright.

Of course, much of the information regarding the history of business flying came firsthand from the aviation professionals who, through their involvement in NBAA, have been industry leaders. Key figures included: E. Ward Akins, Donald A. Baldwin, Donald E. Baldwin, Janice K. Barden, John B. Bean, Robert E. Breiling, Raoul Castro, Ronald J. DeSerrano, Raleigh E. Drennon, E.E. Dunsworth, William F. Gilbert, Malcolm S. Graham, Howard V. Gregory, George E. Haddaway, D.U. Howard, Dennis G. Keith, Harry C. McCreary, Charles O. McKinnon, Scott E. Miller, Charles E. Morris, Cole H. Morrow, Walter C. Pague, Preston S. Parish, Otto C. Pobanz, Lee L. Robbins, Philip A. Roberts, Joe B. Sasser, David M. Sheehan, D.M. Teel, John T. Tucker, Richard J. Van Gemert, David L. Vornholt, William B. Watt, Virgil L. Williams and David M. Woodrow.

Among the dozens of other business aviation industry people who shared their unique recollections and personal perspectives were: Forest Beckett, Max Bleck, Francois Chavatte, James C. Christiansen, John Cummings, Tom Ferranti, Stanley Green, J. Lynn Helms, Russell W. Meyer, Jr., Henry Ogrodzinski, Allen E. Paulson, Roger Ritchie, Kevin Russell, Richard Santulli, John Sheehan, Robert Showalter, Ken Snodgrass, Edward W. Stimpson, Edward J. Swearingen, James

B. Taylor, A.L. Ueltschi, Bruce N. Whitman, Stuart Willmott and John Zimmerman.

Others who provided valuable information and photographs included: Bill Barber, Ron Crotty, Bill Cutter, Walter W. David, Garth Dingman, Norbert Ehrich, Susan Hamende, Rachel R. Haymes, Doug Herman, Betty F. Hinds, John H. House, Jay McDonald, Mary Miller, Bonnie O'Neil, Kay Piper, Joe Playford, Jane E. Rovolis, Carolyn Schlegel, Kelly B. Scott, Bob Smith, Shelly Snyder, Tom Walsh, Mike Welton, John Whitmer and David D. Yeoman. Pat A. Zerbe deserves special mention for fulfilling multiple requests for information.

The contributions of freelance photographers Marianne Barcellona, Paul Bowen, Paul Brou, David Esler, Warren Green and Mike Vines were vital, and a number of museums, including the National Air & Space Museum (NASM), provided unique images that have been used in this book. I am grateful to NASM's Dorothy S. Cochrane, Melissa Kaiser, Kristine Kaske and Brian Nicklas for their efforts. I also must recognize Joan A'Hearn of the Schenectady Museum Association, Ginny Edmonston of the Piper Aviation Museum Foundation, Hazel Stitt of the Dwight D. Eisenhower Library and Karen Thiessen of the College Park Airport Museum.

The historical perspective I gained by researching and writing *B/CA's* "Reflections" column for the past decade proved important when it came time to write *NBAA's Tribute to Business Aviation.* And so was the advice and support of the following people who have been associated with B/CA magazine: Richard N. Aarons, David W. Ewald, Mal Gormley, Arnold Lewis, J. Sheldon "Torch" Lewis, Robert L. Parrish and Archie Trammell.

Other aviation writers, editors and publishers who helped in various ways included: David Collogan, Jack Elliott, William Garvey, James Holahan, Richard Koenig, J. Mac McClellan, Nigel Moll, Murray Q. Smith and Scott Spangler. Al Struna of *Flying* magazine deserves special thanks for handling numerous photo requests.

The logistic, administrative, editorial and legal support provided by Diana Berardinelli, Sally Buswell, Mark Drought, Susan Munsat, Ellen Patafio and Eleanor Searles was important, too. Thanks also to Colorcraft of Virginia for a fine printing job.

It's hard to imagine how this book could have been put together without the contributions of five very important people. John H. Winant graciously reviewed the manuscript and offered the kind of sage advice that made him an outstanding industry leader. David M. Perry lent his unique artistic talents to the design and layout of the book. *B/CA's* Gordon A. Gilbert, who makes a living paying attention to detail, made sure that the text and photographs were consistent and accurate. Robert B. Parke, using his 45 years of experience in aviation publishing, interviewed many of the business aviation leaders and offered expert counsel on how to bring the concept to fruition. Finally, my wife, Mary, exhibited the infinite patience that spouses of authors need to have.

Robert A. Searles
July 1997

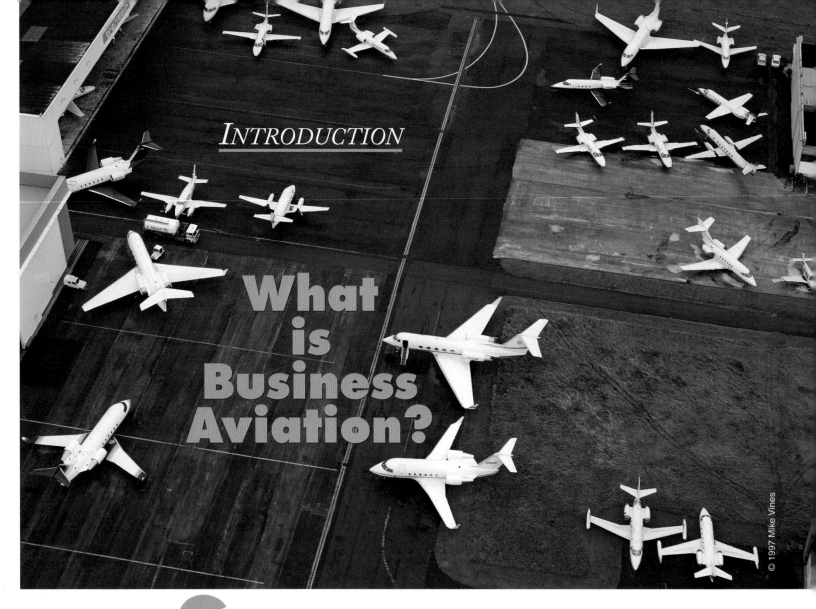

INTRODUCTION

What is Business Aviation?

General aviation includes all aircraft not flown by the airlines or military. Business aviation is the segment of general aviation that consists of aircraft used for business transportation.

Business operators range from individuals who fly rented, single-engine, piston-powered airplanes, to sales or management teams of corporations, many of which own fleets of multi-engine, turbine-powered aircraft and employ their own flight crews, maintenance technicians and other aviation support personnel.

Many companies use business aircraft for transporting priority personnel and cargo to a variety of far-flung locations, including sites overseas. Often business aircraft are used to bring customers to company facilities for factory tours and product demonstrations. Some individuals, such as salespeople and doctors, use business aircraft to cover regional territories. While the overwhelming majority of business aircraft missions are conducted on demand, some companies have scheduled operations, known as corporate shuttles, which essentially are in-house airlines.

Most corporations that operate business aircraft use modern, multi-engine, turbine-powered jets, turboprops or helicopters certified to the highest applicable standards. Aircraft built specifically for business use vary from four-seat, short-range, piston-powered airplanes to multi-engine corporate jets that can carry up to 19 passengers over 6,500 nautical miles non-stop. Some companies even use airline-type jets.

Business aircraft operated by larger companies usually are flown by two-person, professionally trained crews. Smaller operators of business aircraft, especially people who pilot their own piston-powered aircraft, typically use one pilot. Although the majority of business aircraft are owned by individuals or companies, aircraft also are utilized through arrangements such as chartering, leasing, time-sharing, interchange agreements, partnerships and aircraft management contracts. An increasingly popular option is fractional ownership, an arrangement under which a company or individual purchases a one-eighth, one-quarter or larger share of a business aircraft. This entitles the fractional share owner to use an aircraft for a certain number of flight hours each year.

Business aircraft generally are not flown for hire. Thus, the majority of U.S.-registered business aircraft are governed by Part 91 of the Federal Aviation Regulations (FARs). U.S.-registered business aircraft that can be flown for compensation are regulated by FAR Part 135, which covers on-demand commercial operations.

Regardless of how business aircraft are utilized, they are chosen because they provide safe, efficient, flexible and reliable transportation.

Of all the benefits of business aircraft, flexibility is probably the most important. Companies flying aircraft for business purposes can control virtually all aspects of their travel plans. Itineraries can be changed instantly, and business aircraft can be flown to thousands more destinations than are served by the airlines.

Business aircraft allow passengers to conduct business en route in complete privacy while reducing the stresses associated with airline travel: missed connections, lost baggage, overbooking, and worries about air carrier maintenance or security standards. In recent years, business aircraft have compiled a safety record that is comparable, and in some years superior, to that of the major airlines.

The benefits of using business aircraft fall into 10 categories:

1. **Time savings**—Business aircraft not only reduce flight time by providing point-to-point service, they decrease total travel time because they are able to utilize smaller airports closer to final destinations. Also, the office environment of a business aircraft allows travel time to be productive time.

2. **Flexibility**—People who travel by business aircraft do not have to alter their schedules to conform to those of commercial carriers. Consequently, they have the freedom to change course en route and leave and arrive according to their own schedules.

What is NBAA?

The National Business Aviation Association (NBAA), established in 1947, is dedicated to increasing the safety, efficiency and acceptance of business aviation.

NBAA represents the interests of more than 4,700 Member Companies that primarily own, operate, build, or support approximately 6,000 business aircraft. NBAA Member Companies employ more than 19 million people worldwide and earn annual revenues in excess of $4 trillion—a figure that is equal to about half the U.S. gross national product.

For half a century, NBAA has been the primary representative of business aviation before federal, state and local governments. NBAA also participates in major aviation-community forums as well as international activities related to business aviation.

NBAA supports the daily flying activities of Member Companies by providing technical expertise and up-to-date information on safety and other important issues and regulations. In addition, the Association offers publications, seminars, conferences, workshops and forums that focus on business aviation issues. The NBAA Annual Meeting & Convention is the largest purely civil aviation exhibition in the world.

3. **Reliability**—Business aircraft are built to the highest standards, and companies that maintain their own aircraft have complete control of the readiness of their fleets.

4. **Safety**—In recent years, business aircraft have compiled a safety record that is comparable to or better than that of the major airlines.

5. **Improved marketing efficiency**—Business aircraft not only extend the reach of a sales force, they can quickly and easily bring customers to the point of sale.

6. **Facilities control**—Business aircraft help management extend its control by facilitating personal visits to remote company sites.

7. **Personnel and industrial development**—The mobility that business aircraft gives company employees can accelerate training, orientation and teamwork.

8. **Privacy and comfort**—Conversations on business aircraft are confidential, and cabins can be configured to accommodate any special needs of passengers.

9. **Efficiency**—Business aviation enables a company to maximize its two most important assets: people and time.

10. **Security**—A company that uses business aviation can control all aspects of its air travel.

The intangible benefits of business aviation—enhanced management productivity and better customer relations—are difficult to quantify but are no less significant than direct financial return on investment.

PREFACE

The National Business Aviation Association, Inc.—known for the first six years of its existence as the Corporation Aircraft Owners Association, Inc. and for the next 43 as the National Business Aircraft Association, Inc.—is proud to present this chronicle of business aviation's emergence as an integral part of our nation's air transportation system.

Entrepreneurs saw the potential of using company-owned aircraft for business transportation shortly after Charles Lindbergh's 1927 nonstop flight from New York to Paris. With considerable effort by many aviators and business leaders over the ensuing 70 years, business aviation has become an ordinary travel option for thousands of companies worldwide. No longer a novelty or special privilege for top executives, business aviation in 1997 is accepted as a tool that enables management to obtain maximum productivity from its two most important assets, people and time.

At the occasion of its 50th Anniversary, NBAA documents the beginning and evolution of business aviation in the eight chapters that follow. We salute the men and women who nurtured this uniquely American phenomenon that has migrated to all parts of the globe, and we honor the many individuals who served the needs of the business aviation community, particularly during the five decades of NBAA's existence.

We trust this book will be educational to readers who may not be familiar with business aviation, be informative as well as pleasurable to those who are, and be a source of pride to the many dedicated managers, aviators and maintenance personnel who have made business aviation such an important national asset.

NBAA's Board of Directors, its Standing Committees and Professional Staff extend their sincere thanks to the many people who have made this book possible. Business aviation would have neither significance nor history without the many pioneer aviators and businessmen and women who believed in the value of using general aviation aircraft for business transportation. Nor would NBAA exist without their leadership.

We give particular thanks to authors Robert A. Searles and Robert B. Parke for their knowledge of the business aviation community, for their skill in documenting business aviation's heritage and for their dedication to *NBAA's Tribute to Business Aviation*. We also thank Kathleen Hull for her management of this project on behalf of NBAA.

John W. Olcott
July 1997

Chapter 1: A New Business Tool Takes Wing

Charles Lindbergh sparked America's enthusiasm for flying with his transatlantic flight of 1927, and Walter Beech produced many of the aircraft—including the Travel Air, Staggerwing and Beech 18—that companies used to transport people in business aviation's early years.

A New Business Tool Takes Wing

Prior to Charles Lindbergh's solo transatlantic flight in May 1927, most people thought of aviation as a stunt or a technological feat to be marveled at, but certainly not an activity that had any bearing on their everyday lives. Only a small fraction of the general public had flown with a barnstormer, the itinerant fliers who roamed the United States during the 1920s and 1930s, selling airplane rides to make a living. And until commercial air service blossomed after World War II, airline flights were too expensive for all but the most affluent.

Flying was more a novelty than a practical means of transportation for the average citizen prior to World War II. However, Lindbergh's successful crossing of the Atlantic convinced the general public that airplanes finally

Phillips Petroleum's first aircraft flew out of Bartlesville, Oklahoma on behalf of the company's Aviation Fuels Division.

Long Beach Air

Long Beach's Daugherty Field was Southern California's first municipal airport. The facility, which was named after 1920s barnstormer Earl Daugherty, remains an important stop for business aircraft today.

had become sufficiently safe and reliable and that the future belonged to the air-minded.

How did the business community respond to this groundswell of interest in aviation? Some companies were at first unsure whether the airplane could serve as a business tool. However, a number of ingenious entrepreneurs had already used aircraft to promote their products.

Back in 1910, when most people still had not even seen an airplane, let alone flown in one, Max Morehouse, president of a dry-goods store in Columbus, Ohio, figured that his business could benefit from the public's curiosity about aviation. He hired the Wright brothers to transport two packages of silk from Dayton to Columbus and conduct a flying exhibition after the goods were delivered. For weeks before the November 7, 1910 event, newspapers carried daily updates on the upcoming "aeroplane express." Interest was so great that several thousand people each paid $1 to see a Wright Model B biplane perform the world's first commercial air cargo flight.

It wasn't long before companies interested in tapping the public's fascination with flying began buying airplanes for promotional purposes instead of just renting them. In 1919, the Heddon Company of Dowagiac, Michigan, painted the fuselage of its JN 4-D Curtiss Jenny biplane (a popu-

Flying magazine

Jimmy Doolittle, who headed Shell Aviation's flight department in the 1930s, brought the company's Lockheed Vega in for a fuel stop at Lambert Field in St. Louis during a transcontinental trip.

lar surplus World War I training aircraft) to look like a fish to promote its line of fishing lures. About the same time, Simmons Hardware Company of St. Louis began using its Curtiss Oriole biplane to drop sales literature from the skies and transport salesmen to hardware stores.

However, widespread transport of business people by air did not occur until after Lindbergh's epic flight. But once convinced that aircraft were safe enough to carry executives, many companies began increasing the productivity of their top officials by engaging in "industrial aid" or "executive" flying. The A. W. Shaw Company, a Chicago publisher that flew its

Texaco numbered each of its aircraft. This Stinson Jr., designated Texaco No. 3, was operated by the company between 1929 and 1930 from Chicago's Palwaukee Airport, which today is an important center for business aviation in the Midwest.

Texaco

The DuPont Flying Field near Wilmington, Delaware was a cradle of American aviation in the 1920s. Shown here is Atlantic Aviation's first hangar.

Oil companies used the rugged, three-engine Ford Trimotor to transport company personnel and customers and to promote their products and aviation in general.

own Stinson cabin monoplane, explained in *The Magazine of Business* why using a company aircraft to transport executives made sense:

"Like hundreds of other businesses, large and small, the problem of transportation is a vital one with us. Business moves fast these days, and the time of a major executive is very valuable. In the past, executives have been limited to as much travel as available transportation facilities have permitted in a given number of hours. The airplane seems to offer a faster and more flexible mode of transportation, a means of traveling from Chicago to Cleveland, for example, in a little over three hours, whereas by train, the trip requires approximately eight hours. At this rate, in a single day, if necessary, an executive might visit Cleveland, Akron, Canton and Buffalo, or as many other cities in a different direction."

Because of their need to cover breaking events, newspapers, radio stations and motion picture companies were among the first to utilize aircraft in their daily operations. Some newspapers used airplanes to deliver editions swiftly to outlying areas. For example, *The New York Times* flew newspapers

to Florida during the winter and to upstate New York, Vermont, New Hampshire, Maine and Canada during the summer. Other big-city dailies and newspaper chains that utilized business aircraft during the 1920s and

An Airplane That Meant Business

H. L. Ogg, president of the Automatic Washer Company of Newton, Iowa, named his company airplane *Smiling Thru*, but as the words on the door of the Travel Air airplane implied ("Private Air Office of H.L. Ogg"), this airplane was all business.

Powered by a 300-hp Wright Whirlwind engine and featuring an electric starter, Bendix brakes, navigation lights and night flying equipment, the Travel Air was state of the art in the late 1920s. Outfitted with plush velour reclining seats, the cabin featured a dictating machine and a desk on which a portable typewriter sat. Three interior dome lights illuminated the interior so passengers could work at night. A washroom and toilet were installed aft, along with a baggage compartment. An intercom was installed so Mr. Ogg could speak with the uniformed pilot in flight. Perhaps most important, the cabin included an electrical outlet for the dictating machine and provision for charging up to four of the company's washing machines for product demonstrations.

Photos: *Business & Commercial Aviation* magazine

1930s included Gannett, the *Chicago Tribune, New York Evening World, Boston Herald Traveler, New Orleans Times-Picayune* and the *Des Moines Register-Tribune.* Even smaller newspapers, such as Ogden, Utah's *Standard Examiner,* found airplanes useful.

Despite the high visibility of aircraft owned by the media, oil companies were the most prominent users of business aircraft prior to World War II. The L.M.C. Drilling and Producing Company of Wichita was one of the first to put an aircraft into operation when it started flying a Laird Swallow to drilling sites in mid-1921. By the early 1930s, virtually all the major oil companies—including Cities Service, Conoco, Mobil (Socony-Vacuum), Phillips, Richfield, Shell, Standard Oil and Texaco—operated fleets of aircraft to support drilling, exploration and refining activities, as well as to transport executives and conduct sales promotions.

The Standard Oil Company of Indiana took delivery of a Ford Trimotor on May 21, 1927, the day Lindbergh landed in Paris. The company used the three-engine airplane to perform an inspection tour of its Texas oil fields, covering 3,000 miles in 33 hours flying time and completing the job in four and a half days, a trip that company officials estimated would have required nearly two weeks if done using ground transportation.

Texaco's Trimotor flew a number of goodwill tours, including one through the South and Southwest in 1928, a 41-day journey that introduced more than

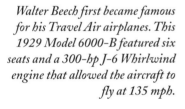

Walter Beech first became famous for his Travel Air airplanes. This 1929 Model 6000-B featured six seats and a 300-hp J-6 Whirlwind engine that allowed the aircraft to fly at 135 mph.

Flying magazine

1,300 people—including several senators, governors and community leaders—to business aviation.

Continental Oil began using aircraft in 1928 when its chairman sold his personal airplane to the company for $1. The following year Conoco obtained a Lockheed Vega and a Travel Air, which became part of the flight department established by E.W. Marland, one of the first aviation managers to perform an aircraft cost justification study.

Lindbergh's transatlantic feat had encouraged many other pilots to attempt to set speed, distance and endurance records in the 1930s, and many of the leading air racers of the era were sponsored or employed by oil companies.

Famous fliers associated with these firms included Jimmy Doolittle of Shell, Texaco's Frank Hawks, Al Williams of Gulf Oil, Edwin Aldrin of Standard Oil of New Jersey, Gilmore Oil's Roscoe Turner, Dudley Steel of Richfield Oil and Art Goebel of Phillips Petroleum.

Besides capitalizing on the publicity of having famous fliers on the payroll, oil companies wanted to promote aviation and their aviation gasolines and lubricants. In addition, a company airplane proved valuable when miles of oil and gas pipelines needed to be inspected or repaired, or when a crew needed to be sent quickly to extinguish an oil rig fire.

By the mid-1930s, all types of industrial corpo-

Texaco Inc., Aviation Transport Services

Shell Oil Company

Top: During the 1930s, oil companies hired noted racing pilots, such as Texaco's Frank Hawks, to run their flight departments.

Bottom: Before and after World War II, Jimmy Doolittle was a member of Shell Oil Company's flight department. In between, he became a national hero for leading the first U.S. air raid on Japan.

National Air & Space Museum, Smithsonian Institution Photo No. 97-15347

Ford's Contributions to Aviation

The Ford flight department was established in 1941, but the car company's involvement with aviation began in 1909, when Henry Ford financed the installation of a Model T engine in a Bleriot airplane. Although that venture was unsuccessful, it didn't dampen his enthusiasm for aviation.

Both Henry Ford and his son Edsel believed that the airplane could be as important to America as the automobile. Because cars and aircraft had common parts and production methods, they saw aircraft manufacturing as a logical extension of their core business. Consequently, in 1923 they each invested $100 in the Stout All Metal Airplane Company. By July 1925, Ford took control of the aircraft manufacturer and sold the initial Ford-built airplane to Philadelphia retailer John Wanamaker.

In 1926, the first of the famous Ford Trimotors was built. The high-wing, three-engine aircraft combined the Fokker Trimotor design with the corrugated skin and all-metal construction pioneered by Junkers. The first Ford Trimotor was delivered in 1927, and a total of 196 were built through 1933.

Henry Ford believed personal aircraft were important, too, so he sponsored development of the Flivver, an experimental single-engine monoplane first flown in 1926.

Ford also was an early operator of business aircraft. America's first company airline took off on April 13, 1925 when the *Maiden Dearborn*, a Stout airplane powered by a Ford-built Liberty engine, carried mail and auto parts between Dearborn, Michigan and Chicago. The air service reportedly saved $1,250 a day in postage, and the success of the operation helped Ford win an air mail contract for the Dearborn-Chicago-Cleveland route.

In addition, Ford helped promote aviation. In 1925, the company sponsored the first Ford Air Reliability Tour, a contest held annually through 1931 to help convince the public that the airplane was a dependable form of transportation. Beginning in 1927, Ford also conducted a national advertising campaign to foster aviation.

In 1924, Ford Airport in Dearborn became the first U.S. field to have concrete runways. Three years later, the facility had the first radio-range navigation unit, which was developed by Ford. By 1930, the company held 35 aviation patents on equipment including brakes, shock absorbers, lights and superchargers.

Despite all these aviation activities, Henry Ford reportedly only flew once in his life. In August 1927, Charles Lindbergh gave Henry a ride in the *Spirit of St. Louis*.

The Great Depression ended Ford's involvement in commercial aviation. However, during World War II, the company produced 8,600 B-24 Liberator bombers and 57,000 aircraft engines. In fact, some of the Ford pilots who test flew B-24s also made some of the company's first executive flights.

8

S.C. Johnson & Son operated a variety of different business aircraft during the late 1920s and early 1930s, including this Waco QDC airplane.

rations were beginning to realize that aircraft, if properly managed, were cost-effective business tools. Naturally, all the airframe manufacturers, as well as a number of aviation instrument and accessory makers, had their own business aircraft.

Even companies whose primary business was other forms of transportation recognized the value of aviation.

The Missouri-Pacific Railroad was one of the first such companies to become a business aircraft user. In addition, the first aircraft produced by the Travel Air Manufacturing Company, one of the earliest airplane manufacturers in Wichita, went to O.E. Scott, a St. Louis auto dealer whose initial flight was to visit Henry Ford.

Left: During the 1930s, Fairchild produced a series of high-wing, single-engine aircraft whose enclosed cabins made flying more comfortable for pilots and passengers alike.

Right: RCA's Fred King owned the 1931 Bellanca Air Cruiser known as Miss Fidelity. *The 15-passenger aircraft evolved from the military C-27 Airbus design.*

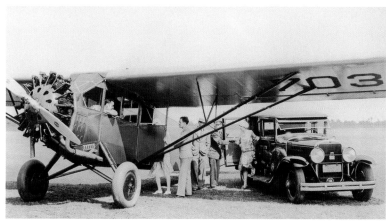

National Air & Space Museum, Smithsonian Institution, Photo No. 97-15348

Flying magazine

NBAA

Although the world's first modern airliner—the Boeing 247—was only operated by major airlines for a few years in the mid-1930s, companies including Hoechst Celanese flew the twin-engine, all-metal aircraft into the 1940s.

The Ford Motor Company itself, in addition to having a fleet of aircraft and its own airport in Dearborn, Michigan, manufactured the famous Trimotor airplane. Also, Ford pioneered the corporate air shuttle concept, initially flying freight between Dearborn and Chicago in 1925. Likewise, General Motors was heavily involved in aviation and had a stake in several aircraft makers, including Fokker Corporation of America.

Other early corporate operators of aircraft included: Parker Pen, Wildroot Hair Tonic, Reynolds Tobacco, Kohler, Kellogg and the

By the late 1930s, the DC-3 had revolutionized airline travel. After World War II, when large numbers of surplus military versions of the aircraft became available, many businesses utilized the large-cabin airplanes for company transportation.

National Air & Space Museum, Smithsonian Institution, Photo No. 75-6504

Youngstown, Ohio Board of Trade, which made business flying affordable for its members by asking them only to reimburse the organization for the actual cost of aircraft operation.

In addition, timber and mining companies, ranchers and farmers, and doctors and salesmen discovered the utility of business aircraft. In almost every case, the basic reason for utilizing an aircraft in business was the same: a company airplane was a "time machine" that would allow business people to get more accomplished each day.

As the Great Depression deepened, however, only prosperous companies and people could afford to purchase and operate aircraft. Because the captains of industry and affluent individuals often flew the same type of well-appointed aircraft for both business and personal transportation, private aircraft developed a reputation of being a luxury, a misperception that legitimate operators of business aircraft have been struggling to overcome for decades.

Part of the confusion arose because the aircraft manufacturers of the era were selling the same products to airlines, businesses and individuals alike. In some cases, transport aircraft makers, such as Boeing, Douglas, Fokker, Grumman and Lockheed, were competing for customers with companies that produced smaller airplanes, such as Bellanca, Fairchild, Stinson and Waco.

Indeed, many of the airliners designed by the transport manufacturers of the 1930s also were used as business aircraft. Several versions of the Lockheed Electra, notably the Model 10 and Model 12 airliners, found their way into the business fleet.

Also, the Boeing 247, known as the world's first modern airliner, was flown by a number of companies, including Phillips Petroleum. The twin-engine, all-metal aircraft, which first flew in 1933, boasted a host of modern features, including cowled engines, variable-pitch propellers, adjustable trim tabs, deicing boots, an autopilot, a two-way radio, six-foot-tall cabin and a lavatory. Most important, the Boeing 247 was 50 percent faster than the leading airliner of the time, the Ford Trimotor.

But as good as the Boeing 247 was, it was soon eclipsed by the faster Douglas DC-3, perhaps the most popular aircraft of all time. More than

The Classic Beech Model 17 Staggerwing

The most enduring and numerous of the early, large single-engine business airplanes was the Beech Model 17 Staggerwing, which initially flew in November 1932. The first design produced by Walter Beech's Beech Aircraft Company, the five-seat biplane was built from 1932 through 1948. The first model was sold to Ethyl Corporation in 1933 for $17,000.

Flying magazine

The Staggerwing, so named because the upper wing was located farther back on the fuselage than the lower wing, was designed to fly at 200 miles per hour. Powered by a number of modern engines, ranging from a 225-hp Jacobs up to the 710-hp Wright Cyclone, the well-appointed aircraft was often referred to as a flying limousine. But it was its high-speed performance and ability to fly 1,000 miles nonstop that made it a favorite among business and military customers alike.

10,000 units were built beginning in 1935, and hundreds were used by business aircraft operators, especially after World War II, when cheap surplus military models became readily available.

It wasn't until after the war that landplanes had the range to cross the oceans safely. Prior to that, commercial carriers with long overwater routes relied on amphibians or flying boats, particularly those made by Grumman and Sikorsky. These aircraft were also popular among corporate operators and wealthy individuals because of their large cabins and ability to land on the waterways near city centers. In fact, more than a dozen businessmen during this period used flying boats to commute to New York City's Wall Street from their homes on Long Island, contributing to the unfortunate image of luxury.

Businesses also employed another specialized aircraft of the 1930s: the autogiro, a vehicle that is powered by a conventional propeller, but supported in flight by a freewheeling horizontal rotor that provides lift. Models manufactured by Kellett and Pitcairn were used by businesses that needed an aircraft that could take off and land in a short distance.

By the end of the 1930s, the three major manufacturers that would specialize in producing piston-powered airplanes built for business aviation—Beech, Cessna and Piper—had emerged from the Depression while many other manufacturers had faded.

Flying magazine

Fairchild was one of several manufacturers that opted to produce high-wing aircraft, which gave the pilot an unobstructed view below the airplane. This four-seat F-24 was powered by a 175-hp Ranger engine.

Bottom Left: *Beginning in the mid-1920s, Detroit-based Stinson was noted for producing single-engine aircraft that featured soundproofed and heated cabins, engine starters and wheel brakes. The Reliant model shown here had a graceful tapered wing.*

Bottom Right: *In major cities situated next to waterways, bases for seaplanes and amphibians afforded convenient access to downtown, an important consideration for time-conscious businessmen.*

National Air & Space Museum, Smithsonian Institution, Photo No. 97-15349

National Air & Space Museum, Smithsonian Institution, Photo No. 97-15345

Although their timing seemingly couldn't have been worse, Walter Beech, his wife Olive Ann, and a few associates decided in April 1932 to start the Beech Aircraft Company. Their objective was to design and build a five-place biplane with a luxury interior, a top speed of 200 mph or better, a landing speed of 60 mph or less, and a nonstop range of approximately 1,000 miles. The now-famous Model 17 Staggerwing made its first flight in November 1932 and stayed in production until well after World War II.

Within a few years, Beech launched another successful aircraft, the all-metal, twin-engine Beech 18. The eight-place airplane had wide appeal among airline, military and corporate customers. The venerable Twin Beech stayed in production for more than 30 years and was a mainstay of the business fleet from the 1940s through the 1960s.

Clyde Cessna, who had been building aircraft since before World War I, started a new airplane company in 1934 with his son Eldon and nephew Dwane Wallace. Cessna's most successful design of the 1930s was

Before creating the first practical helicopter in 1939, Igor Sikorsky was renowned for his flying boats and amphibians. This Sikorsky S-38C was flown by S.C. Johnson & Son during the mid-1930s.

Bottom Left: Walter J. Kohler, CEO of Kohler Company for more than two decades and governor of Wisconsin from 1928-1930, flew regularly in this Brougham, which was made by Ryan, the company that produced Lindbergh's Spirit of St. Louis.

Bottom Right: One of the most popular of the high-speed Howard DGAs ("damn good airplanes") was the Model 15. The DGAs earned their reputation in part because of the air racing prowess of founder Benny Howard.

NBAA

National Air & Space Museum, Smithsonian Institution, Photo No. 80-15994

Hall of History Foundation, Schenectady, NY

General Electric's (left to right) E.G. Haven, W.W. Miller and A.H. French stand next to the company's first airplane, which was based at Schenectady, NY beginning in December 1931.

the Airmaster, a high-wing monoplane that was touted as the "most efficient airplane" and flown by a number of companies. A few years later, Cessna added a successful twin-engine business aircraft designated the T-50.

Piper Aircraft Corporation, founded in Lock Haven, Pennsylvania by William T. Piper, Sr. in November 1937, won a following with its simple J-3 Cub. The company went on to build 130,000 airplanes, including a variety of single- and multi-engine business aircraft.

During this period, a number of technical innovations advanced the state of the art in aircraft design and enhanced the acceptance of business aviation. The introduction of aircraft with enclosed cabins was an important step forward in the late 1920s. The move from heavy, liquid-cooled reciprocating engines to lighter, more powerful and reliable air-cooled radial powerplants also was significant. By the mid-1930s, the Sperry automatic pilot and Hamilton Standard constant-speed prop made flying easier, and the

Long before New Jersey's Teterboro Airport became a hub of business aviation in the New York metropolitan area, barnstormers, such as Gates' Flying Circus, performed aerial stunts at the field.

Photo: *Business & Commercial Aviation* magazine

Oil companies, such as Phillips, and other Staggerwing operators liked th[e] aircraft's 200-mph speed. Engines used on the Model 17 ranged from a 2[...] hp Jacobs radial up to the 710-hp Wright Cyclone.

NB

The Spartan Executive, one of the first all-metal business aircraft, entered service in the mid-1930s. However, less than three dozen of the sleek single-engine aircraft were built before the Tulsa-based manufacturer closed its doors in 1946.

advent of cabin pressurization in 1937 made travel by air more comfortable. Superchargers helped boost engine performance, and before the decade was through, the first practical helicopter and jet-powered aircraft gave a glimpse of what lay ahead for business aviation.

The Legacy of Walter and Olive Ann Beech

No husband and wife team had a greater impact on business aviation than Walter and Olive Ann Beech. During his 30-year career as a pilot, instructor, engineer and manufacturer, Walter was a leading advocate of the business airplane. Following his death in 1950, Olive Ann took the reins of the Beech Aircraft Company, the firm they had founded together in 1932, serving as its chairman for more than three decades.

Tennessee-born Walter Beech was an Army flight instructor in World War I who came to Wichita, Kansas in 1921 to serve as a test and demonstration pilot for the locally built Laird Swallow airplane.

By 1924, Walter Beech decided to form his own aircraft firm, the Travel Air Manufacturing Company. The only woman and nonpilot among the company's dozen employees was Olive Ann Mellor, a secretary and bookkeeper.

"When I started working at Travel Air, I didn't know the empennage of an airplane from the wing," she conceded. But her business acumen soon won her the job of office manager, and she often flew with Walter, whom she married in 1930.

By 1929 Travel Air had become the world's largest commercial aircraft maker. The company merged with Curtiss-Wright, and Walter relocated to New York City. But soon he yearned to build his own aircraft again, so in 1932, he returned to Wichita. Along with Olive Ann and several other former Travel Air associates, he founded the Beech Aircraft Company, which has produced some of the most famous business aircraft, including the Staggerwing, Beech 18, Bonanza and King Air.

When an illness sidelined Walter for nearly a year in 1940, Olive Ann led Beech Aircraft. And after Walter passed away in 1950, she became president and chairman of the board, a post she held until 1982. In 1981, she joined her husband in the National Aviation Hall of Fame, making them only the second couple, after Charles and Anne Lindbergh, to be so honored.

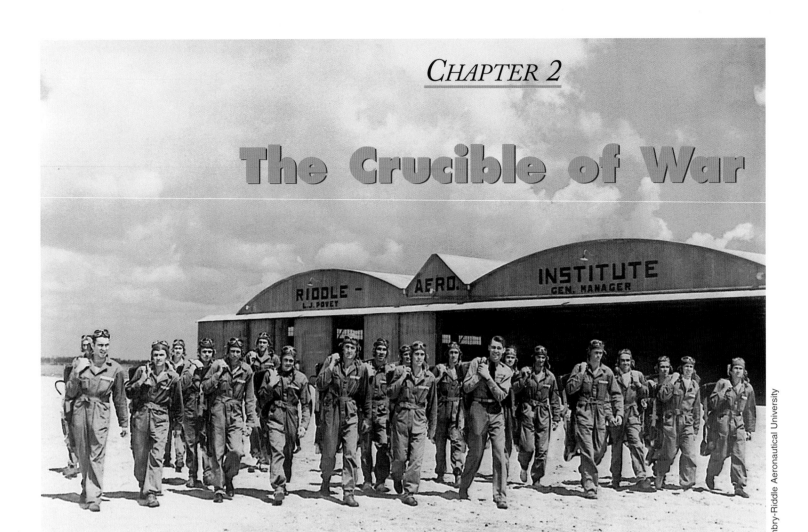

Embry-Riddle Aeronautical University

CHAPTER 2

The Crucible of War

The Riddle Aeronautical Institute was one of the many civil flight training organizations that taught thousands of young men how to fly immediately before and during World War II.

By the late 1930s, as the United States slowly started to pull out of the Great Depression, aviation mirrored some of the growing optimism in the country. Airline travel was expanding, subsidized by air mail contracts and made more comfortable and profitable by modern transports, such as the Boeing 247 and Douglas DC-3.

General aviation also was on the rise. Many ordinary people, once content to vicariously experience the exploits of record-chasing aviators, began to consider the idea of climbing into the cockpit themselves. The accidents that claimed the lives of famous pilots such as Wiley Post and Amelia Earhart served as reminders that flying still could be dangerous. But the record-setting round-the-world flight of Howard Hughes and the transatlantic triumph of Douglas "Wrong Way" Corrigan, who crossed the ocean in a simple single-engine airplane, inspired many to take to the air.

The introduction of affordable and easy-to-fly general aviation aircraft, such as the Piper Cub, made it possible for these people to realize their dreams to fly. In addition, new, more-capable twin-engine aircraft,

16

The Douglas C-47, the military version of the DC-3 airliner, was used for a variety of roles during World War II, including glider towing. Converted C-47s were popular among business aircraft operators after the war.

McDonnell Douglas

such as the Beech 18 and Cessna T-50, were aimed at meeting the transportation needs of a growing number of air-minded businessmen.

Aviation companies known as fixed base operators (FBOs) provided the support these new operators needed. From cities such as Columbus, Ohio, where Lane Aviation was located, to the small town of DeWitt, Iowa, home of Elliott Aviation, FBOs supplied private and business fliers with a variety of services, from flying lessons and aircraft rentals to equipment repair and fuel.

In 1938, the federal government recognized the growing importance of aviation by establishing a separate agency, the Civil Aeronautics Authority (CAA), to regulate the industry. While the CAA was primarily concerned with regulating commercial aviation, the new agency's chairman, Edward J. Noble, declared, "The whole question of private flying needs immediate and special attention." Therefore, in December 1938, the CAA's Federal Private Flying Section was established.

The main task of the Private Flying Section was to simplify regulations and reduce unnecessary restrictions on general aviation. Less conspicuous, but perhaps more important was a CAA initiative to examine how private flying could be developed as an asset to other industries. This effort

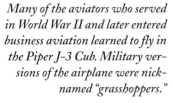

Many of the aviators who served in World War II and later entered business aviation learned to fly in the Piper J-3 Cub. Military versions of the airplane were nicknamed "grasshoppers."

Piper Aviation Museum

included collecting accurate aircraft-operating cost data, studying how airplanes were utilized in product distribution and selling, and determining the airplane's possible effect on the decentralization of business.

Although the Private Flying Section wanted to help nurture emerging business and private operators, Noble noted that, unlike the airlines, the general aviation community did a poor job of communicating its needs to the government. Noble told two friends, Laurence and Philip Sharples, that the only input he received from non-commercial operators was via ad hoc groups that often had conflicting positions. Noble suggested that it would be helpful if there were an organization that could coherently articulate the views of general aviation operators.

Consequently, the Sharples brothers—along with Alfred Wolf, C. Townsend Ludington and John Story Smith—formed the Aircraft Owners and Pilots Association (AOPA) in early 1939. Ever since, AOPA has clearly and forcefully stated the needs and desires of individuals who fly general aviation aircraft.

While America was getting back on its economic feet and U.S. general aviation enjoyed a surge of popularity in the late 1930s, much of the rest of the world was facing a rising tide of fascism that would eventually lead to another global conflict. After World War I, many U.S. leaders—even the revered Lindbergh—were convinced that isolationism and neutrality were the keys to preventing America from getting drawn into a second world war. Ignoring the pleas of a few vocal military leaders, such as air power advocate General Billy Mitchell, America let its air forces wither. However, after Hitler demonstrated the power of the Luftwaffe during the Spanish Civil War and annexed Austria and Czechoslovakia, it became clear that appeasement of the Nazis was futile. America began to mobilize.

The first move to bolster U.S. military aviation capability came in September 1938. President Franklin D. Roosevelt set an annual production goal of 10,000 military aircraft. Two months later, he unveiled the Civilian Pilot Training Program (CPTP), a plan to train 20,000 college students each year to fly in order to create a reservoir of pilots for the armed services.

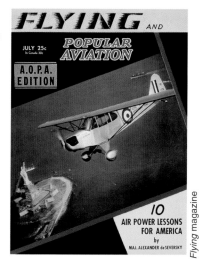

Flying magazine, which began covering general aviation in 1927, devoted a section of the publication to news about the Aircraft Owners and Pilots Association after the group was founded in 1939.

During World War II, more than 90 percent of all U.S. bombardiers and navigators learned their skills in the AT-7 navigation trainer and the AT-11 bombing and gunnery trainer, both of which were military models of the Beech 18.

Most of the airmen who earned their wings under this program learned to fly in Piper J-3 Cubs.

A number of FBOs capitalized on this business opportunity, including Mountain States Aviation, which had been founded in Denver in November 1938 by Harry Combs, who later became president of Learjet. Between 1941 and 1944, Mountain States trained 9,000 pilots.

The number of American pilots was mushrooming, as was the number of general aviation aircraft in the U.S. fleet, thanks in part to the promotional

Olive Ann Beech poses in front of a UC-43, the military version of the company's Staggerwing.

activities of the light airplane manufacturers. Piper placed advertisements in magazines such as *The Saturday Evening Post* and each week gave away a Cub to one of 40,000 contestants who listened to the "Wings of Destiny" radio program. In addition, Aeronca, Luscombe and other manufacturers offered free flight instruction as an incentive to aircraft buyers.

The number of airports was expanding, thereby increasing the usefulness of general aviation aircraft for business and private operators alike. New, easier-to-fly types were available, such as the Ercoupe, which featured a simple, automobile-like control system. And other airplane models were upgraded with onboard radios and other equipment designed to improve their safety and utility. These enhancements were reflected in an improving safety record.

But the specter of world war hung over the future of business and personal flying. By 1940, a growing number of military and government leaders questioned how helpful general aviation would be to the military if America had to go to war.

Granted, the CPTP had increased the pilot pool, but the program had its detractors, even within the aviation industry. Some called it just

Approximately 40 Cessna T-50s were sold before the war to private operators such as Bill Lear. Beginning in 1940, over 5,000 trainer versions of the wooden aircraft were produced for the military.

William T. Piper, Sr. helped convince the armed services that general aviation airplanes could be used in military operations. The Piper Cub and other light aircraft were used in a variety of roles during World War II.

National Air & Space Museum, Smithsonian Institution, Photo No. 87-6033

another New Deal boondoggle. Isolationists were suspicious of any program with military overtones, and the armed forces were not enthusiastic about trusting civilian instructors to train future military pilots. In addition, implementation of the program had not been as smooth as advocates had hoped. Criticism of CPTP grew, and flight schools quickly realized that their training contracts were in jeopardy.

The fledgling FBO industry decided to organize to save their bacon. Led by Roscoe Turner, a former air race pilot and flight school operator, and George Haddaway, the publisher of *Southern Flight* magazine, 200 industry representatives convened in Kansas City in December 1940. There they resolved to fight for continuance of CPTP and formed an organization that would become known as the National Air Transportation Association. After the Japanese attack on Pearl Harbor, however, all non-military flying in the United States, except for scheduled airline operations, ceased.

Although America was at war and limited raw materials had to be devoted to the production of military aircraft, the general aviation industry mounted a campaign to convince the federal government that properly directed private flying was essential. The defense-related functions that could be performed best by light planes—patrol, medical evacuation and transport of key defense personnel—were touted.

The PBY Catalina, a long-range patrol and bomber aircraft that became famous during the Battle of Midway, was later used by business aircraft operators who needed the ability to land on both water and land.

NBAA

Finally, in early 1942, the ban on general aviation activity was lifted. But before pilots could have their licenses reinstated, they had to prove their citizenship and loyalty. An extensive system of flight clearances was established at each airport. Initially, no cross-country flying was permitted, but eventually business and pleasure flights with pre-approved flight plans were allowed. When hangared, aircraft had to be disassembled to prevent use by saboteurs.

General aviation aircraft operators who wanted to help defend America joined the Civil Air Patrol (CAP), the paramilitary organization that was founded in December 1941. A quarter million volunteers performed a variety of duties, including flight-testing air defense systems, ferrying pilots to aircraft factories and, most importantly, patrolling the Eastern seaboard in search of German submarines.

Meanwhile, builders of business aircraft were busy trying to meet President Roosevelt's revised goal of churning out 50,000 U.S. military aircraft per year, a massive undertaking that earned American industry the title "Arsenal of Democracy." Thousands of fighters and bombers were needed, but the first priority was to build advanced training airplanes. These advanced trainers needed to be fabricated from non-strategic materials so that vital resources could be conserved for use in front-line aircraft. Wichita's major general aviation manufacturers responded by building two

The Ercoupe, which featured a simple, automobile-like control system, was one of the single-engine general aviation aircraft mass produced immediately after the war. Some 4,000 Ercoupes were built in 1946 alone.

College Park Airport Museum

Military Aviators Get Down to Business

Many of the young men who flew during World War II later became the first postwar business aircraft pilots. Through their long and distinguished careers in aviation, these veterans helped define business flying and its leading organization, the National Business Aviation Association (NBAA).

Ralph E. Piper founded Monsanto's flight department following World War II.

Walter C. Pague was an original member of the NBAA Board.

Otto C. Pobanz led Federated Department Stores' aviation department for 30 years.

One man who helped organize the Corporation Aircraft Owners Association (the original name for NBAA) was Walter C. Pague. Upon leaving the Navy in 1945, he was hired by American Rolling Mill Company (ARMCO) to fly the Midwestern steel company's new Twin Beech. Recognizing the challenges that he and other business aircraft operators were facing, Pague was involved with NBAA activities from the inception of the Association in 1947 until his retirement from ARMCO in 1980. He was an original member of the NBAA's Board of Directors, serving until 1964. He also helped create NBAA's first working group, the Technical Committee, which was founded to help keep operators abreast of the latest aircraft maintenance and service needs and techniques.

Another man who founded a flight department was Monsanto's Ralph E. Piper, a former civilian and Army flight instructor who during the war flew Douglas C-54s over "The Hump" (the air route that stretched over the Himalayas from India to China). Piper initially was a partner in the St. Louis aviation service company founded by Bill Remmert and Bob Werner. But when Monsanto chairman Edgar Queeny asked him to set up a company aviation operation, Piper signed on for what would be a 21-year stint with the chemical maker. Following his retirement, he became an author and consultant. He was an NBAA Director from 1952 through 1958.

Otto C. Pobanz also was a flight instructor, first as a civilian and later in the Navy. After the war, he flew Douglas transports throughout the Americas for a non-scheduled carrier, then piloted a DC-3 for RCA. He is best remembered, however, for the 30 years he spent with the aviation arm of Cincinnati-based Federated Department Stores. Beginning in the early 1970s, Pobanz served on the NBAA Board for more than a decade.

Charles E. Morris ran Mobil Oil's flight operations for more than two decades.

After flying anti-submarine patrols over the Atlantic and combat missions in the Pacific, Charles E. Morris began an airline career with Pan Am in 1946. Within five years, however, he decided to try his hand at flying a DC-3 for Socony-Vacuum Oil Company, which later became Mobil. Four years later, Morris was named manager of Mobil's worldwide aviation operations, a post he held for more than two decades. While amassing 10,000 hours

aloft, he still managed to find time to serve on the NBAA Board from 1967 through 1979.

William B. Watt flew for a number of leading corporations and was affiliated with Atlantic Aviation and Executive Air Fleet.

William B. Watt, a North American B-25 pilot during the war, hooked up with ITT after leaving the service in 1945. Not only was Watt ITT's first chief pilot, he was involved in test flying some of the company's radar and instrument landing system equipment. Later, he served as chief pilot for Hoover, AT&T and Atlantic Aviation before helping found Executive Air Fleet, a pioneering aircraft management company, in 1965. Watt's involvement in NBAA activities dates from the 1960s, and today he is a business aviation safety consultant.

twin-engine airplanes that were manufactured primarily of wood: The Beech Model 25/26 Wichita and the Cessna T-50 Bobcat.

During the war, Cessna constructed more than 5,000 AT-8s, the military version of the T-50. Beech built over 2,300 units of the Model 26 (AT-10), which was similar to the Beech 18, thousands of which were flown by the U.S. Army and Navy for a variety of missions. The most notable military Model 18s were the AT-7 navigation trainer and the AT-11 bombing and gunnery trainer. During the war, more than 90 percent of all U.S. bombardiers and navigators honed their skills in these two aircraft. In addition, some 500 Beech Staggerwings flew for the Allies, mostly as personnel transports.

Not content to merely provide basic trainers, single-engine airplane manufacturers also sought military aircraft production contracts. At their own expense, Aeronca, Piper and Taylorcraft provided the Army with airplanes in order to demonstrate that light aircraft were well-suited to perform aerial observation and other missions.

Beginning in September 1941, the U.S. military ordered more than 5,000 Piper Cubs, most under the designation L-4 (for liaison). Cubs and other light general aviation aircraft were used for aerial photography, medical evacuations, locating and picking up downed pilots, laying telephone wire, and airlifting food, blood and ammunition.

Although helicopters would not join the business fleet until years later, rotorcraft played a role, albeit minor, in World War II. In May 1942, Sikorsky delivered the XR-4, the prototype for the first helicopter produced in quantity for the U.S. armed forces.

In the final analysis, World War II transformed America, its aviation industry and its people. In 1939, U.S. factories manufactured fewer than 6,000 aircraft; by 1944, wartime requirements had boosted annual aircraft production to nearly 100,000 units. Defense needs also spurred development of new and improved aviation technology, such as turbine engines, radar, transponders and navigation aids. Air power had been a decisive factor in winning the war, and aviation was to prove crucial to postwar U.S. economic development.

Thousands of young American military pilots and mechanics who went overseas returned home with aviation skills and a desire to fly. Armed with G.I. Bill benefits (which gave them reimbursement for civil flight training), they were confident that they could meet the challenges of civil aviation. Even veterans who did not pilot or maintain aircraft had seen how effective airplanes could be, and many were eager to fly for business or pleasure.

But the aviation industry's transition to peace was anything but smooth. At the end of the war, the military canceled $9 billion worth of contracts, including orders for 31,000 aircraft. Nearly a half million factory workers were laid off within two weeks. Some aircraft manufacturers were forced to develop non-aviation products to keep their people occupied.

The Airplane That Jump-Started Postwar Business Flying

The availability of surplus, low-cost military aircraft and an ample supply of pilots who had cut their teeth on these airplanes during World War II were major factors in the emergence of business aviation in the late 1940s.

Perhaps no model was more important to the postwar growth of business flying than the Douglas DC-3 and its military counterpart, the C-47. Between 1935 and 1946, Douglas built more than 10,000 of these rugged twin-engine transports.

Noted for its large cabin, reliable twin radial engines and ability to routinely perform feats such as over-gross takeoffs and 500-foot landings, the DC-3 quickly became the workhorse of the business fleet. Between 1941 and 1946 Douglas delivered a few new DC-3s to companies. However, hundreds of converted DC-3s and C-47s were sold by modifiers such as St. Louis-based Remmert-Werner, Miami's L.B. Smith, PacAero and AiResearch in California, Mallard Industries in Connecticut and Horton & Horton in Texas.

Initially priced at less than $100,000, by the mid-1950s some of these remanufactured airplanes cost upwards of $250,000, more than twice the cost of the original 1935 DC-3. Still, these reliable, familiar aircraft were a bargain for the hundreds of companies that bought them for business transportation.

The Douglas DC-3 was the flagship of the postwar business aviation fleet. Hundreds of DC-3s and surplus C-47 military versions were flown by companies, including Gannett, during the 1950s and 1960s.

Flying magaz

Be-Ge Manufacturing was among the smaller companies that flew the single-engine Ryan Navion. The all-metal, four-place airplane, which was introduced in 1946, featured dual controls, a powered retractable tricycle gear and steerable nose wheel.

Initially, it appeared as if the pent-up demand for civil aircraft might fill the void. By early 1946, over 30,000 aircraft were registered in the United States, with 40,000 more on order. Although 21,000 combat planes had been scrapped, hundreds of Army and Navy transport aircraft, including C-47s (the military version of the DC-3), were sold as surplus and converted for airline or business use. America had 140,000 licensed pilots, many of them veterans who earned their civil wings thanks to the G.I. Bill, and the CAA was issuing student certificates so fast that it lost count of how many had been handed out.

Not wanting to miss the postwar boom, general aviation manufacturers rushed prewar models back into production and prepared new ones for the bumper crop of civil customers. Piper produced 1,000 Cub Specials between the armistice and the end of 1945, and production of the popular two-place taildragger peaked at 50 per day in June 1946. Beech developed a new version of the Model 18 that went from flight test to production in 60 days, making it the first postwar business aircraft to receive a new type certificate. By December 1945, the company had started flight testing the Model 35 V-tail Bonanza, which would prove to be another popular business airplane. Cessna had two new metal airplanes, the Model 120 and 140, in the works, and new or reworked designs were being offered by Aeronca, Bellanca, Fairchild, Luscombe and Taylorcraft.

Military aircraft makers, such as Republic and North American, introduced light airplanes of their own. Even aviation equipment manufacturers, such as Bendix, developed aircraft for the seemingly insatiable market. Light airplanes were being produced and sold like automobiles. In fact, their mass appeal was deemed so great that major department stores such as Macy's, Marshall Field and Wanamaker's began selling them.

Perhaps no airframe manufacturer exemplified the boom and bust cycle of 1946 better than Engineering and Research Corporation (ERCO), maker of the Ercoupe. The company delivered 71 aircraft in 1945. By the summer of 1946, the manufacturer had 14,000 orders in hand and was building 10 airplanes per day. By September, the bottom fell out of the market, and within two months, the production line was closed.

While aviation manufacturers suffered through this roller coaster environment, many businesses established their company flight departments during this era, taking advantage of the availability of low-priced ex-military aircraft. One such company was Eastman Kodak, which obtained a surplus C-47 in 1945 because airline flights did not serve the smaller cities where its people needed to go. The only other public transportation option was rail service, which in some cases took days to reach towns such as Kingsport, Tennessee, where Eastman Kodak had a major facility.

Republic, which was renowned for its World War II fighter aircraft, also developed the Seabee, a four-place, all-metal amphibian that entered service in the late 1940s.

Although the federal government promised to spend large sums of money on development of new airports and navaids, the air transportation system was ill-equipped to handle the rapid postwar growth in civil aviation. Consequently, the prospect of continuously overcrowded skies, jammed runways and delayed flights prompted regulators to consider rationing airspace and landing rights. The aviation pie was about to be divided, and Palmer J. (Bud) Lathrop, an executive with Bristol-Myers Company, and Sydney Nesbitt, president of Atlantic Aviation Corporation, were concerned about how such restrictions might affect business aircraft operators.

Said Lathrop, "We operate an airplane which is of tremendous aid to our executives, and we want this operation to remain successful. The success of the 'industries aid' operations depends upon whether or not rules are

National Air & Space Museum, Smithsonian Institution, Photo No. 12282

made which will make it difficult for us to give the officials of our companies the services we wish. Decisions are being made now which can seriously affect our operations in the future."

In order to marshal support for equitable treatment of business aviation, Lathrop and Nesbitt called a meeting at the Wings Club in New York City, and the 13 men who met there on May 17, 1946 decided what was needed was an organization that would promote and protect the interests of business aviation.

Lathrop wrote to a number of companies that operated aircraft, inviting them to send an emissary to a second meeting that was to be held in conjunction with the Cleveland Air Races of 1946. The 25 representatives who showed up on November 21 agreed to launch the Corporation Aircraft Owners Association (CAOA) "to protect [business aviation] interests from discriminatory legislation by federal, state and municipal agencies...to enable corporation aircraft owners to be represented as a united front...[to foster] improvements in aircraft, equipment and service...and to further the cause of safety and economy of operation."

The most popular and fastest of the new single-engine general aviation postwar aircraft was the Beech Bonanza. The V-tail airplane made its first flight in December 1945.

Flying magazine

On February 13, 1947, CAOA was incorporated in New York as a not-for-profit group, and the organization held its first annual business meeting in New York's Biltmore Hotel on September 24 of that year.

Eighteen "voting" (aircraft operating) companies were members by then: American Rolling Mill, Bristol-Myers, Al Buchanan Drilling, Burlington Mills, Champion Paper and Fiber, Corning Glass Works, General Electric, B.F. Goodrich, Goodyear, Hanes Hosiery Mills, Howes Brothers, National Dairy Products, Republic Steel, Reynolds Metals, Sinclair Refining, L.B. Smith Inc., United Cigar-Whelan Stores and Wolfe Industries. The first and, at that time, only Associate Member was Atlantic Aviation.

It would be several years before the business aviation community and CAOA (which changed its name to the National Business Aircraft Association in 1953 and the National Business Aviation Association in 1997) would develop the critical mass to influence national aviation policy. But from this modest beginning, they were on their way to becoming an integral part of the country's air transportation system.

Atlantic Aviation of Wilmington, Delaware, the first NBAA Associate Member, became a major service center for business aircraft after World War II, distributing both Beech and Piper aircraft.

Atlantic Aviation

During the 1950s, L.B. Smith modified and serviced military and airline surplus Douglas DC-3s for use as business transports.

Business Aviation's Formative Years

Just as the Berlin Airlift of 1948 exemplified how the United States, the leader of the Free World, could use its military air power to draw a line in the sand against Communism, Cessna President Dwane L. Wallace suggested that aviation could play a crucial role in the postwar growth of domestic commerce.

"The expansion of the personal plane to its fullest potential can mean a great deal to the national economy," declared Wallace. "Every major surge in the growth of our national economy has coincided with the introduction

Especially during business aviation's formative years, companies flew the same type of transport aircraft as the scheduled air carriers. This Convair 240 was the first aircraft in Texaco's fleet to have a pressurized cabin.

Texaco

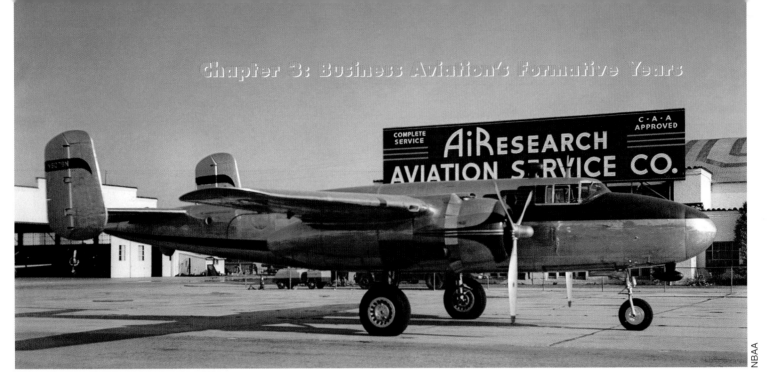

Top: AiResearch Aviation transformed North American B-25 bombers into business transports at its Los Angeles facility.

Right: Scott E. Miller, AiResearch Aviation's head of customer service, inspects the interior of Conoco's North American B-25 shortly after AiResearch finished converting the airplane. In 1964, Miller became the first person to serve as an Associate Member Advisor to the NBAA Board.

of a new method of transportation, and it is significant that each has been a faster method of travel. The airplane presents the next major step forward in fast transportation, and if the proper kind of assistance can be rendered at this crucial time, it may mean the possibility of a tremendous self-sustaining industry."

Wallace stated that the keys to satisfying the pent-up demand for air transportation and unleashing the economic power of aviation would be to improve the utility of general aviation aircraft, develop a nationwide airport system and associated navigational aids, and simplify civil air regulations.

The year 1947 turned out to be a turning point in the development of commercial and general aviation in the United States. The federal government launched a national program to provide the financial assistance necessary for the construction, expansion and repair of U.S. airports. In addition, the International Civil Aviation Organization (ICAO) was created to facilitate the establishment of worldwide standards for aviation safety, reliability and navigation.

The new era in airline operations was symbolized by several events of 1947. Douglas stopped building the DC-3, and Convair flew the Model 240, the first of a family of new airliners. Major air carriers began using long-range landplanes in place of flying boats to initiate new services, including nonstop transatlantic flights. Five years later, the de Havilland Comet inaugurated the turbojet era of commercial aviation, and by the mid-1950s, the British were laying plans to build the world's first commercial supersonic transport.

Bottom Left: Hoechst Celanese began operating this converted Douglas B-23 bomber in 1953.

Bottom Right: Like many pilots who pioneered business aviation during the 1950s, Monsanto's Bob Hinds spent many years with one flight department.

Meanwhile, World War II veteran aviators who entered the burgeoning field of business aviation after the war naturally were inclined to continue flying the same aircraft they had flown during the war, in large part

NBAA

Monsanto

because of the dearth of new aircraft designed specifically for business flying and the ready availability of cheap military surplus equipment. For example, when Jimmy Doolittle returned to the Shell Oil flight department, he flew a converted North American B-25 bomber. Other companies adapted Convair B-24s, Douglas A-26s and B-23s, Lockheed PV-1s, Martin B-26s and other ex-military aircraft for business transportation. The versatile Grumman amphibians, such as the Widgeon, became popular company transports as well. However, the favorite multi-engine business airplanes were the Beech 18 and the DC-3 (and its C-47 military version).

The Beech 18 cockpit was the "front office" for hundreds of business aviation pilots who flew the popular twin-engine aircraft during the 1950s.

One of the leading designers who helped convert military aircraft to business use was Dave Ellies, who in 1955 began crafting interiors for DC-3s and other surplus airplanes. Some of the shops that specialized in modifying these airplanes included Remmert-Werner of St. Louis, Horton & Horton in Texas, Miami's L.B. Smith, PacAero and AiResearch in California and Mallard Industries of Connecticut. Companies with limited needs for air travel utilized single-engine general aviation airplanes, both pre-war models and new airplanes such as the Beech Bonanza, North American Navion and Republic Seabee.

Those Who Teach Flying Can Do!

FlightSafety International's A.L. Ueltschi.

In March 1951, a 34-year-old corporate pilot for Pan American Airways started a side business that has grown into a billion-dollar industry and made the skies safer for everyone.

A.L. Ueltschi, a Kentucky-born former barnstormer, figured that business aviators needed the same type of thorough and disciplined training that airline pilots received, so he founded FlightSafety International.

Operating initially from a single room at New York City's LaGuardia Airport with only a wooden desk, a typewriter and a secretary, FlightSafety offered to train a business aircraft operator's pilot and copilot for $750. The package included a primer on aircraft systems, air traffic control procedures and aviation regulations. Flight instruction, which was provided by moonlighting airline pilots, was done in two stages: first on a rented United Airlines Link trainer based at LaGuardia, and then in the customer's airplane.

For the first several years, business was slow. With FlightSafety only earning a net profit of $277 on revenues of more than $177,000 in 1955, Ueltschi couldn't afford to give up his day job as a pilot for Pan Am. In fact, during that year, the company had to sell five-year training subscriptions in order to finance the acquisition of its own simulator. However, by the end of that decade, the company was a million-dollar-a-year business with 50 employees providing training for pilots of 200 corporations.

The need for instruction in the turbine-powered business aircraft introduced in the early 1960s made FlightSafety International a resounding success, and Ueltschi finally retired from Pan Am in 1968 to devote all his energies to the training company.

Nearly 30 years later, Ueltschi sold FlightSafety International for $1.5 billion, having collected numerous personal awards (including the Wright Memorial Trophy and NBAA's Meritorious Service to Aviation Award) for his achievements. Today, FlightSafety provides training for ship captains and operators of power-generation facilities while teaching 50,000 pilots and technicians annually how to fly and maintain more than 50 different types of aircraft.

The Cessna 310 was an example of a new class of light, twin-engine general aviation aircraft introduced in the 1950s.

Also, a new generation of light, two-engine, general aviation aircraft was developed for companies that needed more range and passenger-carrying capacity or desired the redundancy provided by dual engines and systems. In 1946, Ted Smith formed Aero Design and Engineering to produce the Aero Commander, which entered service in 1952. Turboprop- and turbojet-powered versions of this popular high-wing aircraft followed. Piper's first twin-engine airplane, the Apache, entered service in 1954, the Beech Twin Bonanza first flew in 1949, and the Cessna 310 took to the air in 1953.

The late 1940s and early 1950s were also an important time for development of rotary-wing aircraft. In 1946, the Bell 47 became the first helicopter to receive a commercial type certificate from the Civil Aeronautics Administration. During the Korean War, the so-called "Bubble Bell" developed the art of helicopter rescue operations by airlifting wounded

During the Korean War, the Bell 47 was used to airlift thousands of wounded soldiers to safety. Companies such as Weyerhauser later used the single-engine helicopter in utility operations.

NBAA

The First Business Jet

National Air & Space Museum, Smithsonian Institution, Photo No. 97 15355

The four-seat Morane-Saulnier M.S. 760 was marketed by Beech in the mid-1950s, making it the first non-airline jet used for business transportation.

In 1952, de Havilland launched the turbojet era of commercial aviation with its four-engine Comet airliner. Nearly a decade would pass, however, before the first turbojet-powered airplanes marketed for business aviation would join the fleet in significant numbers.

But back in 1955, Beech tried to jump ahead in the race to field a business jet by acquiring the North American distribution rights to a four-place French jet known as the M.S. 760 "Paris." Built by Morane-Saulnier, the four-place, low wing, T-tail aircraft featured two 1,000-pound-thrust engines, tip tanks and a sliding canopy.

A Paris jet demonstrator was shipped by freighter to New York City and then trucked to Westchester County Airport in White Plains, New York, where it was assembled. Be-

ginning in June 1955, Thomas W. Gillespie (who later became an executive with Piper Aircraft) and several other pilots spent the next 90 days making more than 700 demonstration flights during a nationwide tour.

Although U.S. airlines were in the process of placing $1 billion worth of orders for jet transports, business aviators were worried that this new type of aircraft might be too expensive or difficult to operate. The M.S. 760 had a top speed of more than 400 mph, but its engines were loud, takeoff performance was lackluster and its range left something to be desired.

Only a few of the $250,000 aircraft were sold, one of which went to Ohio industrialist Henry Timken. After several years of marketing, Beech gave up selling the M.S. 760 and dropped its option to produce the aircraft under license.

FBOs and Aircraft Operators: Partners in Service

In aviation's earliest days, mechanics drove under the intended flight path of an aircraft so that they could be ready to service the airplane wherever it might set down. By the mid-1920s, aircraft had become reliable enough that mechanics could wait to service aircraft at a permanent facility, which gave rise to the term fixed-base operator (FBO). Flight training became a major part of of the aviation business just before and during World War II, but after the war, fueling and serving the other needs of business aircraft became the focus of many FBOs.

Older pilots will recall that most FBOs of the late 1940s looked pretty scruffy. Often they were makeshift facilities, usually with a dingy building, simple fuel pump and a dirt parking area. However, some FBOs began to recognize that if they were to survive and prosper in the postwar era, it was time to spruce up. By the mid-1950s, many were trying to attract business aircraft by being the classiest, most service-conscious outfit in town.

Among the first to establish "red carpet" service for business aircraft were Atlantic Aviation of Wilmington, Delaware; Lane Aviation in Columbus, Ohio; Cutter Aviation in Phoenix; Beckett Aviation in Youngstown, Ohio; Showalter Aviation in Orlando; Southwest Airmotive of Dallas and Hawthorne Aviation based in Charleston, South Carolina. In those days, dispensing name-brand fuel, along with outstanding service, often was the key to attracting business aircraft. In fact, major oil companies encouraged their dealers to set and maintain high standards, which led to the creation of specially designated facilities, such as Phillips Aviation Performance Centers.

As it turned out, intense competition for what was a relatively small market prompted some mammoth oil companies to exit the retail aviation fuel business by the 1970s. But even as major oil companies left the business, independent FBOs

with a good reputation at one airport began to set up bases at other fields. Combs Aviation in Denver, Page Aviation of Rochester, Chicago-based Butler Aviation, Aero Services of Teterboro, New Jersey and Beckett Aviation of Youngstown, Ohio all successfully opened facilities at other locations.

The consumer expected and usually received a consistently high level of service from each of these affiliated FBOs, and owners or managers of individual facilities enjoyed the advantage of joint marketing and promotion.

The consolidation of the aviation service industry in recent years has led to the establishment of "super chains," such as Signature Flight Support or the independently owned and operated network of Million Air FBOs, both of which have dozens of facilities operating under a common banner.

Today, hundreds of modern FBOs across the United States support the needs of business aircraft and their passengers, 24 hours a day, 365 days a year. Dozens more first-class FBOs are located overseas, as business aviation spreads its global wings.

Periodically, the relationship between business aircraft operators, which have grown accustomed to prompt, top-notch service and facilities, and FBOs, which aim to provide amenities as well as essentials at a cost that allows them to make a profit, has been strained. Some FBOs have instituted "ramp fees" to cover the cost of the free services they provide, while some aircraft operators try to ease an FBO's financial burden of providing such extras by buying "courtesy fuel." Such gestures underscore the fact that FBOs and aircraft operators need each other in order to provide the highest quality air transportation.

Fixed-base operators that specialized in maintaining and servicing general aviation aircraft were key to the growth of business flying in the 1950s.

Cessna Aircraft

The Cessna 190 was one of the new, all-metal, single-engine airplanes introduced after World War II.

soldiers to field hospitals. Companies soon discovered that light helicopters could also be used effectively to transport personnel and supplies directly to factories, construction sites and remote areas that were inaccessible by either airplane or automobile.

One of the centers of business aviation on the East Coast is Westchester County Airport in White Plains, New York. Built originally as a base from which interceptor aircraft could defend New York City from enemy air attacks, the field was converted to civilian flying after World War II.

Westchester County Airport

By the mid-1950s, Aerospatiale and other rotorcraft manufacturers had outfitted helicopters, such as this Alouette II, for business transport missions.

Eurocopter

43

An FBO Pioneer

After World War II, Forest Beckett was one of the first people to open an FBO dedicated to business aviation. His Youngstown, Ohio facility was the first of a chain that included bases in Cleveland, Chicago, Houston, Palm Beach, Phoenix and Pittsburgh.

Forest Beckett pioneered the concepts of aircraft leasing, interchange and management during the 1950s and 1960s.

For three decades, Beckett FBOs were recognized for their standout environment and service, as well as for several innovative programs that made owning and using business aircraft easier. One was to structure aircraft exchange agreements between companies so they would not be defined as charter operations. That way, a company could use an aircraft of another company for certain flight operations while paying only the costs of the airplane for those missions. Beckett also pioneered aircraft leasing and aircraft management services in the 1950s and 1960s.

After 30 years, Beckett sold his aircraft service centers in 1978. But a few years later, he re-entered the business by establishing Beckett Enterprises at Cleveland's Cuyahoga County Airport.

New aircraft electronics (called "avionics"), instruments and equipment were developed to make flying easier, especially in reduced visibility and severe weather. For instance, during the 1950s, many commercial and general aviation operators began installing airborne weather radar so that they could either fly around storms or choose to penetrate weather fronts at their weakest point.

A June 1948 survey of Corporation Aircraft Owners Association (CAOA) Members revealed how business operators were outfitting and operating their aircraft during that era. The poll showed:

• A majority of companies flew with a pilot and a copilot, one of whom was a qualified mechanic.

• Most single-engine aircraft operators only flew those aircraft during the day. However, average monthly multi-engine aircraft utilization was 55 hours per month, which included eight hours of instrument flying and 11 hours of night operations.

New Jersey's Teterboro Airport has been home base for many leading operators of business aircraft, including Texaco, which built a hangar there for its Executive Aircraft Division in the mid-1950s.

Photos: Dwight D. Eisenhower Library

- Very High Frequency (VHF) radios were installed in 82 percent of aircraft, and 70 percent of the operators polled preferred using a combination of Ground Controlled Approach (GCA) and Instrument Landing System (ILS) equipment.
- All multi-engine aircraft were fitted with deicing equipment and vacuum-operated flight instruments. Three quarters had dual altimeters, airspeed indicators and compasses. Nearly half had autopilots.

Generally, the most sophisticated business aircraft operators installed the same state-of-the-art systems that airlines did. But a number of companies

Top: This Aero Commander, which was operated by the U.S. Air Force, was the first general aviation aircraft used to regularly transport the President of the United States. Dwight D. Eisenhower often utilized the aircraft to fly between the nation's capital and his home in Gettysburgh, Pennsylvania

Right: Dwight D. Eisenhower, who was the first U.S. President to ride in a helicopter, learned the value of on-demand air transportation while serving as a U.S. Army general in Europe during World War II.

Flying Big Blue

One of the business aviation pioneers who founded an aviation department for a major corporation during the 1950s was Charles O. McKinnon, the highly respected aviator who ran IBM's flight operation from 1954 to 1977.

Charles O. McKinnon founded the IBM flight department in 1954.

A World War II veteran and graduate of the Civilian Pilot Training Program at Georgia Tech, where he earned an engineering degree, McKinnon flew DC-3s for United Airlines after the war. One day in the ready room, he noticed a recruitment ad that was seeking someone to start a flight department for a large U.S. corporation. The company turned out to be IBM, and one of the tests for aviation department manager candidates included flying with the company's chairman, Thomas J. Watson, Jr., who McKinnon called "one of the best stick and rudder people I ever flew with."

McKinnon got the job, and the company's first airplane was an Aero Commander 500. Later, IBM acquired Gulfstream II business jets and established the first European-based flight department for a U.S. company. During the initial year of operation, IBM Paris flew to more than 100 destinations in Europe, the Middle East and Far East.

The venerable Beech 18, commonly known as the Twin Beech, stayed in production for more than 30 years and was a mainstay of the business fleet from the 1940s through the 1960s.

that operated aircraft were not content to adapt military and airline airplanes; they challenged manufacturers to develop airframes, engines and equipment specifically tailored to business flying. At an August 1948 CAOA

Kerr-McGee was the owner of this Martin B-26 bomber, which the company acquired in 1950.

Business & Commercial Aviation magazine

forum, operators asked for an aircraft that could carry 10-12 passengers, fly well in excess of 200 mph and have one-stop transcontinental range.

Most business airplanes and helicopters continued to be piston powered, but during the 1950s, the first business jet (the Morane-Saulnier M.S. 760), first business turboprop (the Gulfstream I) and the first turbine-powered helicopter (the Kaman K-225) took to the air.

Meanwhile, aircraft manufacturers continued to improve their piston-powered products. Instrument panels, windshields, control wheels and seats were upgraded to minimize the chance of injury, and a 1950 analysis by Eugene W. Norris, a Cessna distributor, showed that during the previous

Arthur Godfrey, the popular radio and TV personality of the 1950s, often extolled the virtues of flying during his broadcasts. His efforts to promote aviation won him NBAA's Meritorious Service to Aviation Award.

10 years, lightplane performance had improved markedly while operating costs had actually dropped.

The growing international capability of business aircraft was demonstrated between August 7 and December 17, 1949, when a Douglas DC-4 operated by Salem Engineering, an Ohio construction company, made what reportedly was the first round-the-world flight of a business airplane. The aircraft was piloted through 24 countries by Nelson U. Rokes, who went on to fly for Procter & Gamble for more than 25 years. Salem Engineering President Sam Keener noted that the trip was not made simply for promo-

Conoco, Gannett, Hoechst Celanese and Kelly Springfield were some of the companies that operated the Lockheed Lodestar for business transportation.

tional purposes: "Traveling by private plane to see the potential customer and survey his problems and needs right on the spot is the only way to do business in this field."

By 1951, more and more companies began to recognize the value of business aircraft. Of the estimated 60,000 civil aircraft in U.S. service that year, approximately 18,000 were utilized directly in connection with business, and 8,000 were owned by corporations. Although airline service was becoming more affordable and reliable, only about 500 U.S. cities could be reached directly by scheduled air carrier. Company-owned aircraft and charter airplanes flown by FBOs picked up much of the slack.

In fact, some companies that used aircraft for their own business transportation discovered that there was money to be made supporting fellow aircraft operators. Textile maker J.P. Stevens was a prime example. In the late 1940s, company executive Robert T. Stevens was introduced to

The Irrepressible George E. Haddaway

Those who know George E. Haddaway will be pleased to learn that in 1997, at age 88, he still was his irrepressible self, with a booming voice and nonstop tales about his 60-year career in aviation publishing.

According to Haddaway, he entered the field almost as an afterthought. "After graduating from the University of Texas at Austin in 1930, I couldn't get a job [because] of the Great Depression. So I got a Merchant Marine ticket and went to sea. Went all around the world. Smartest thing I ever did: Got a Ph.D. without going to college," he quipped.

"I had flown a few hours in a Waco 10 at college," Haddaway continued. "Another fellow and I would fly down to Mexico and pick up a few liters of grain alcohol, bring it home and cut it into gin. So in 1934, we figured we were aviators and could start a magazine. In April 1934, we started publishing *Southwestern Aviation*. It was all about business flying, oil companies and the like." The publication was later renamed *Southern Flight* and then simply *Flight*. Haddaway ran the magazine for 44 years.

George E. Haddaway, the publisher of Flight *magazine, was an early and ardent supporter of business aviation.*

During his tenure, Haddaway saw the birth and growth of NBAA. By the time the Association held its annual meeting in Dallas in 1954, he was co-chairman of the Convention. Haddaway has been a fixture at NBAA annual meetings ever since, and in 1976, he received the Association's Award for Meritorious Service to Aviation.

The Upjohn Company

Virgil L. Williams, longtime NBAA Director and chief pilot for The Upjohn Company, began his career with the firm in 1959 as a copilot in this Learstar.

business flying by traveling on Pan Am's company airplane, a converted Douglas B-23 bomber. Stevens was so impressed with the comfort and convenience of this mode of travel that in 1950 he decided to acquire his own airplane, a Beech 18. Within a few years, Stevens began pumping fuel and doing emergency repairs for aircraft that stopped at its base in Greenville, South Carolina. By the end of 1962, Stevens Aviation decided to set up an FBO at the then-brand-new Greenville-Spartanburg Airport and eventually became one of the largest operations in the Southeast.

Business aviation was becoming big business and an important part of the national transportation system. To ensure that the industry would have ample opportunity to shape federal aviation policy, CAOA moved its

William P. Lear tested many of his inventions, including the Lear Orienter and Lear Omnimatic, in his Twin Beech flying laboratory.

LEAR ELECTRO-P

LEAR,

50

The Grumman Mallard Miss Daily News *was used by the New York City newspaper to quickly transport reporters and photographers to the scene of breaking news.*

offices from New York City to Washington, D.C. in 1951. Two years later, the organization changed its name to the National Business Aircraft Association (NBAA) to help clarify its mission and activities. That same year, the Association encouraged Member Companies to exhibit products and services at the group's annual meeting and presented safe flying awards for the first time. Within two years, Flight Safety Foundation recognized the unique challenges of business flying and held the first of its annual corporate aviation safety seminars.

NBAA's 1954 Annual Meeting and Convention in Dallas reflected the growing importance of business aviation. The Convention was the group's first three-day gathering and included major technical sessions dedicated to the maintenance and operation of the more popular types of equipment in the fleet of more than 1,500 multi-engine aircraft operated by American companies. Airplanes for sale were displayed at Southwest Airmotive's FBO on Love Field,

Postwar airliners, such as the piston-powered Martin 404, were utilized by business aircraft operators that needed to move a large volume of passengers or cargo.

NBAA

Business & Commercial Aviation Magazine

Just after World War II Continental Oil's fleet at Ponca City, Oklahoma included a variety of aircraft ranging from a Beech Bonanza to a Lockheed Vega and Lodestar.

During the 1950s, Amoco operated several Lockheed Venturas. Dee Howard made a business out of upgrading Venturas, the most notable example of which was his Howard 500.

NBAA

one of the major centers of business aviation activity in the United States.

While the use of business aircraft was growing, the United States and other countries were trying to develop a common airways navigation system for both civil and military operators. The U.S. military was dedicated to its Tactical Air Navigation (TACAN) system, while most civil aviation groups, including NBAA, preferred Very High Frequency Omnidirectional Range/Distance Measuring Equipment (VOR/DME). In 1956, the United States adopted VORTAC, a combination of VOR and TACAN/DME. After a protracted and heated battle with proponents of alternative navigation systems, such as Britain's Decca, VORTAC became the international standard.

The event that perhaps had the most far-reaching impact on aviation during the 1950s was the midair collision of two airliners over the Grand Canyon in June 1956. The accident claimed a record 128 lives and set into

The dozens of aircraft on display at Dallas' Love Field during the 1954 NBAA Convention illustrated the diversity of business aviation. Models shown ranged from new light twins, such as the Cessna 310 and Piper Apache, to airliners, such as the Martin 202 and Douglas DC-3.

NBAA

motion a process that led to a comprehensive review of the air traffic control (ATC) system and the establishment of a new, dedicated independent federal agency to regulate aviation.

As part of the ATC review process, general aviation organizations, including NBAA, were asked to define their future needs for aviation facilities. A dramatic increase in use of aircraft for business purposes, including a substantial rise in instrument flying, was forecast, and federal airport and airways planners were urged to meet the needs of general aviation so it could continue to contribute to the country's economic advancement.

In 1959, the newly created Federal Aviation Agency (FAA), led by a retired general named Elwood "Pete" Quesada, began an overhaul of the aviation system that in the years to come would dramatically change how business aircraft would be designed, built and operated.

Some of the most influential people in business aviation have served on NBAA's Board of Directors. This 1955 photo shows (front row, left to right) Cole H. Morrow, who served as Board Chairman in the early 1950s and later was an FAA executive; Henry. W. Boggess; Joseph B. Burns and Eugene T. Spetnagel. Also pictured (back row, left to right) are Gerard J. Eger; Walter C. Pague, the first Chairman of the Association's Technical Committee; Curt G. Talbot and Robert C. Sprague, Jr.

NBAA

Turbine Power and Controlled Airspace

By the late 1950s, business flying was climbing and poised to fly even higher as it spooled up to enter the Jet Age. Having seen what military and commercial jets could do, companies that operated piston-powered aircraft were encouraged by the possibilities of using high-speed turbine-powered aircraft for business transportation. Within a decade, businesses that had relied on converted surplus airliners and military aircraft could choose from an array of turbine- and piston-powered aircraft—from high-performance single-engine models to sophisticated jetliners—to meet virtually any of their diverse air transportation needs.

Building on the success of its earlier twin-engine, piston-powered aircraft, Aero Commander developed the Model 1121 Jet Commander in the early 1960s. Follow-on versions of the aircraft were produced by Israel Aircraft Industries.

Flying magazine

Top: The Fokker F-27—a high-wing, twin-turboprop airliner produced in the United States by Fairchild—also was a popular business aircraft.

The first type of turbine aircraft to enter the business fleet was the turboprop, an airplane that used jet powerplants instead of piston engines to drive propellers. The Fokker F-27—a high-wing, twin-turboprop airliner that was billed as a DC-3 replacement—was purchased by several dozen companies beginning in the late 1950s. Grumman felt there was enough interest in a business turboprop that it developed the Gulfstream G-159 (later known simply as the Gulfstream I). The G-I, which was the first turbine-powered aircraft specifically designed for business flying, entered service in 1959.

Bottom Left: Collins avionics and ram's horns control yokes were distinctive features of the cockpit of the Hawker Siddeley 125 business jet.

Developed originally by Britain's de Havilland Aircraft and called the Jet Dragon, the Model 125 business jet has been known by a variety of names, but is most often referred to as the "Hawker" because it was produced for many years by Hawker Siddeley.

Collins Avionics

Business & Commercial Aviation magazine

The business jet era began in 1958, when Timken Roller Bearing of Canton, Ohio took delivery of a French-made, four-seat Morane-Saulnier M.S. 760. By the early 1960s, more than a half dozen business jets were being offered, most of which were powered by either General Electric CJ610 or Pratt & Whitney JT-12 turbojets. The most popular models were the Aero Commander 1121 (referred to as the "Jet Commander"), the de Havilland 125 (commonly called "Hawker"), France's Fan Jet Falcon (known later as the "Falcon 20"), the legendary Lear Jet 23 and two converted military transport jets—the North American Aviation Sabreliner and the Lockheed JetStar.

The first of these turbojet-powered business aircraft to enter service was the JetStar, which joined the fleet in September 1961. Two years later, the Sabreliner was flying in civilian dress, followed by the de Havilland 125 and Lear Jet in 1964 and the Jet Commander in 1965. The first business jet to use quieter and more efficient turbofan engines was the General Electric CF700-powered Fan Jet Falcon, which was certificated in 1965, the same year that the first jetliner outfitted for business use (a British Aircraft BAC 1-11 operated by Tennessee Gas Transmission Company) was delivered. By the end of the decade, improved models of first-generation business jets—such as the Dash 8 JetStar, Learjet 24 and 25 and Sabreliner 60—were introduced.

To help operators sort out the performance claims of jet aircraft makers, in 1964 NBAA's Technical Committee developed an instrument

Left: Developed originally to meet a U.S. Air Force requirement for a utility jet transport, the Lockheed JetStar was the leading large turbojet-powered business aircraft of the early 1960s. The four-engine airplane typically was configured to carry 10 passengers.

Right: Noted for its spacious interior, the turbojet-powered Lockheed JetStar stayed in production until the late 1970s, thanks to improvements such as re-engining with more-efficient Garrett TFE 731 turbofans.

NBAA

National Air & Space Museum, Smithsonian Institution, Photo No. 97-15353

Right: J. Sheldon "Torch" Lewis (right), a business aviation pilot and pundit best known for his "Greenhouse Patter" column in Business & Commercial Aviation magazine, confers with Najeeb Halaby (center), FAA Administrator under President John F. Kennedy and later president of Pan Am World Airways, and Gerald Wilmot (left), president of Page Airways.

Signature Flight Support

flight rules (IFR) flight profile for turbojet-powered aircraft. The so-called "jet range format" provided a yardstick by which to measure the capabilities of business jets.

Meanwhile, a new class of smaller business turboprops was developed, the most notable being the Beech King Air, a six- to eight-place,

Bottom: The first Beech King Air made its maiden flight from Beech Field in Wichita on January 20, 1964. The twin-engine aircraft went on to become the most widely used turboprop in the business fleet.

Raytheon Aircraft

twin-engine aircraft that was certificated in July 1964. Within a few years, other light turboprops appeared, including the Japanese-built Mitsubishi MU-2 (which was distributed in the United States by Mooney Aircraft), the Swearingen Merlin and Aero Commander's Turbo Commander. Pratt & Whitney PT6 or Garrett TPE 331 engines were used to power most of these smaller turboprops.

New, lightweight turbine engines for rotorcraft, such as the Allison 250 turboshaft, eliminated much of the vibration common in piston-powered helicopters and gave rotary wing aircraft the power needed to make

A Magazine of Their Own

A young publishing executive named David W. Ewald traveled to the 1957 NBAA Annual Meeting in Denver to assess the possibility of producing a magazine devoted to business flying. The following January, the inaugural issue of *Business & Commercial Aviation (B/CA)* appeared, and the monthly publication has been a leader in the field ever since.

B/CA was founded on the premise that business aircraft owners and pilots need a source of authoritative technical information on new aircraft and equipment, so the publication has specialized in analyzing state-of-the-art airframes, powerplants and avionics. *B/CA* also examines piloting, maintenance and management trends and issues.

The original editorial staff was led by Bill Osmun and included noted writers Harley Kysor and James Holahan. Over the years, such distinguished aviation journalists as Holahan, Archie Trammell, John

W. Olcott and Richard N. Aarons have also served as Editor-in-Chief. Pundits, ranging from Dave Collogan and George Larson to Arnold Lewis, have been B/CA columnists, and ever since 1964, readers have been regaled by the wit and wisdom of veteran business aviation pilot J. Sheldon "Torch" Lewis.

© 1997 Paul Jones

Business & Commercial Aviation magazine.

B/CA's *longtime publisher, David W. Ewald*

Flying magazine

The high-wing, twin-turboprop Mitsubishi MU-2, which first flew in 1963, featured high cruise speeds and good short-field performance.

them productive for business use. The quantum leap in helicopter performance made possible by turboshafts was illustrated by one of the most popular single-turbine models, the Bell 206 JetRanger, which first flew in 1966. The manufacturer claimed that the 206—which had a range of approximately 350 nautical miles and a top speed of about 120 knots—could fly 50 percent farther, 50 percent faster with up to a 50-percent reduction in seat-mile costs, compared to similar-sized piston-powered helicopters.

While turbine power dramatically increased the capability of top-of-the-line business aircraft, the development of turbocharged and pressurized versions of piston-powered light aircraft allowed them to achieve impressive cruise speeds and to climb above bad weather while maintaining a comfortable cabin environment. The first pressurized light twin was Aero Commander's Alti-Cruiser, which was introduced in 1958, the same year that the fuel-injected Beech Twin Bonanza was unveiled. During the 1960s, three-quarters of the light twin-engine aircraft sold were flown by businesses, while air taxi operators opted for higher-capacity medium twins, such as the Piper Navajo, which was first delivered in 1967.

As turbocharging was added to smaller piston engines, high-performance single-engine aircraft were fitted with pressurization systems. One of the most popular of such aircraft was the Cessna 210. Even normally aspirated piston singles, such as the Cessna 172, proved popular, particularly among individual businessmen who flew their own aircraft.

During this era of rapid growth and change in aviation, a new national aviation regulatory body was formed. The Federal Aviation Agency (FAA) took over the functions of the Civil Aeronautics Authority (CAA) and the Airways Modernization Board (a transitional organization created in 1957), as well as the safety regulatory duties (excluding accident investigation) of the Civil Aeronautics Board (CAB). The FAA, which needed to codify existing aviation regulations and write new rules for turbine aircraft, faced an even more daunting task: It had to expand the nation's airports and airways while redesigning the air traffic control (ATC) system and aviation infrastructure to accommodate new, high-performance aircraft.

It was clear from the outset that a major overhaul of the aviation system would cost many millions of dollars. President Eisenhower's budget proposals of 1958 launched what has been a 40-year-long debate on what percentage of the airports and airways system should be funded by users and how much should be paid for by the general public, which benefits from a safe, modern and efficient air transportation system. Over the years, NBAA and business aircraft users have fought unreasonable user charges but have agreed to pay their "fair share" of aviation system costs as long as they have a say in how the money is spent.

Flying magazine

The high-performance, single-engine Cessna 210—which was offered in normally aspirated, turbocharged and pressurized versions—was popular among independent businessmen.

Flying magazine

The four-seat Cessna 172, which was in production for three decades, was a favorite entry-level aircraft of businessmen who were owner-pilots.

NBAA

Top: Luncheon attendees during the 1958 NBAA Annual Meeting probably felt right at home as they sat near a DC-3 parked in this hangar at Philadelphia International Airport.

Bottom: During the 1958 NBAA Annual Meeting in Philadelphia, new aircraft such as the Lockheed JetStar (right) and Grumman Gulfstream (left) not only were on static display, they performed aerial demonstrations that were an integral part of the NBAA trade show until the mid-1960s.

NBAA

While the debate raged over how to fund the revamped aviation system, the FAA conducted a survey of general aviation and sought input from various industry groups in order to determine what facilities and services this segment of aviation would need. Just like a decade earlier, business aircraft operators were worried about getting squeezed out of a crowded aviation system that was likely to be restructured to facilitate commercial and military air traffic.

NBAA President Joseph B. Burns noted in 1958 that the biggest problem facing business aviation was "getting our share of the diminishing airspace. Make no mistake about it, we deserve a share. American business flies the best and most modern equipment, and in greater numbers than any other segment of general aviation. I believe strongly that we've demonstrated a legitimate need for our share of the airspace. And in the future, we'll need more, if for no other reason than that business is the backbone of the country."

B. J. Bergesen, who succeeded Burns as NBAA President in 1959, added that the key would be to utilize airspace more efficiently. "I feel that to have optimum safety, we must continually get a higher percentage of flight activity on a controlled basis."

The FAA, spurred by a series of highly publicized midair collisions and the prospect that such incidents could increase once higher-speed jets entered the aviation system, moved ahead with a new plan for managing air traffic.

In the Beginning of the Turbine Era, There Was a Gulfstream

Grumman earned a reputation for building durable U.S. Navy combat aircraft during World War II. But when the market for carrier-based fighters sagged in the mid-1950s, the Long Island-based airframe maker, affectionately called the "Grumman Iron Works," began looking to exploit new markets.

Following the advice of its chief pilot, Henry J. Schiebel, Grumman developed a business aircraft called the Gulfstream G-159, later known as the Gulfstream I. Powered by two Rolls-Royce Dart turboprops and typically configured to carry 10 passengers, the Gulfstream was the first turbine-powered airplane designed specifically for business aviation. The aircraft first flew in August 1958 and made its public debut one month later at the NBAA Annual Meeting in Philadelphia.

The $700,000 Gulfstream I was certificated in May 1959, and the initial operator was Sinclair Refining. With a pressurized cabin, a cruise speed of more than 300 knots and a range of almost 2,000 nautical miles, the Gulfstream was a popular business transport. Some 200 were built by the time production ended in 1969.

The Grumman Gulfstream G-159 (later known as the Gulfstream I) was the first turbine-powered aircraft specifically designed for business aviation. Two hundred G-Is were produced before the design was superseded by the twin-turbofan-powered Gulfstream II.

NBAA

The Howard 500, a converted Lockheed PV-1 Ventura, was one of the most impressive conversions of a World War II aircraft. The piston-powered airplane had a pressurized cabin and very large fuel capacity.

Many in the aviation industry believed that development of onboard equipment to warn of impending midairs, especially around busy airports, would be a cornerstone of the new ATC structure. But the FAA determined that a workable collision avoidance system was not yet technically feasible, so the agency devoted its efforts to reorganizing the airspace and developing ground-based facilities that could monitor, control and separate air traffic.

A continental control area, terminal traffic areas and three levels of airways (later reduced to two) were established. Control towers and other ATC facilities were set up. Airport surveillance and long-range radars were installed, and precision instrument landing systems (ILS) were put in place at busier airfields. As the new air traffic control system matured, the floor of positive control airspace was lowered.

A key element of the revamped ATC structure, both in the United States and abroad, was the use of VOR/DME (very high frequency omni-directional range/distance measuring equipment), which the International

While New York City's LaGuardia Airport has always been a hub of commercial flying, the field's Marine Air Terminal also has been an important center for business aviation.

Civil Aviation Organization (ICAO) endorsed in 1959 as the worldwide standard for short-range navigation through 1975. During this period, four-course radio-range navigation ground stations began to be replaced by VOR/DME installations (VORTACs).

AlliedSignal Avionics

Top: The King KY-90 VHF communications radio was one of the many successful business aviation avionics products developed in the 1960s by King Radio.

The airlines had hoped that air traffic controllers would be able to use air-to-ground data links as the primary means to exchange information with airborne aircraft, but most communications were accomplished via two-way voice radio. Transponder beacons installed on aircraft helped controllers identify air traffic on their radar scopes, but pilots periodically had to call in to report their position. Within several years, more capable transponders, including one specifically designed for general aviation airplanes, were able to automatically report the altitude and identity of an aircraft, and by the mid-1960s radar coverage was nationwide.

Bottom: During the early 1960s, Cutter Aviation's ramp at Phoenix Sky Harbor Airport was frequented by a variety of aircraft, from single-engine personal aircraft to multi-engine business airplanes.

However, the continuing reliance on voice communications between aircraft and ground facilities soon resulted in congested aviation radio fre-

Cutter Aviation

Top: The PPI-1D indicator was a familiar and often-watched display by pilots who flew with the Bendix RDR-1 radar in the 1960s.

Bottom Left: The Dassault Falcon 20, like most business jets, was equipped with state-of-the-art avionics and equipment. Note the Bendix radar in the middle of the instrument panel.

Bottom Right: Dassault's Fan Jet Falcon was the first production business jet to use turbofan engines, which were quieter and more fuel-efficient than turbojets. Pan American World Airways was the initial distributor of the twin-engine jet in the United States.

quencies. In order to accommodate the communication needs of a rapidly growing aircraft fleet, the FAA told aircraft operators who wanted access to all airspace that they would have to use altitude-encoding altimeters and increasingly sophisticated aircraft radios that featured reduced channel separation. Even before the FAA established minimum equipment requirements to operate in certain airspace, business aircraft operators realized that advanced avionics were needed to receive expeditious handling in the new ATC system.

During the early 1950s, most advanced avionics and other aircraft instruments were designed primarily for airliners and were too large, heavy or expensive to be put into smaller general aviation aircraft. But the application of transistor and microelectronics technology in the early 1960s dramatically decreased the size and weight of avionics while increasing their reliability and reducing their cost.

Equipment such as autopilots, deicing systems and onboard weather radar, which previously were found only in larger aircraft, began appearing in light twins. Likewise, airline-quality navigation and communication

Bill Lear and the Lear Jet

Development of the Lear Jet 23 moved from Switzerland to Wichita during the summer of 1962. After the staff worked six days a week for a year, the Lear Jet 23 was finally rolled out there on September 15, 1963.

Lear Jet 23-006 still looked as good as new when this photo was taken in October 1993, almost 30 years after the aircraft came off the production line.

Business & Commercial Aviation magazine

Learjet

Brilliant inventors usually are not content to rest on their laurels. They are always looking for the next challenge.

Such was the case with William P. Lear in the early 1960s. A tempestuous and unpredictable genius with a fertile mind, Lear had built a company upon his innovative automatic direction finders and autopilots. But he sold his stock in Lear Incorporated so he could finance the development of a new business jet that, although smaller and lighter than any competitive design, would be as fast as any airplane in business aviation.

Lear assembled a multinational team of engineers to develop in Switzerland what was originally called the SAAC 23. When the project bogged down, he decided to move the program to Wichita, where beginning in September 1962 he and his small staff worked long hours on a tight budget to bring the Lear Jet to market ahead of its closest competitor, the Jet Commander.

In a calculated gamble to save money, no prototype was built. The aircraft went straight from design to production. Assembly of the first Lear Jet began in February 1963, and the airplane was rolled out in September of that year. Despite a delay caused by the need to redesign the tail, the Lear Jet flew for the first time on October 7, 1963.

A protracted certification program followed, partly because the first aircraft was destroyed in a mishap in June 1964, but mainly because the FAA had never before certificated a business jet weighing less than 12,500 pounds. Regulators were in uncharted territory, and they made the Lear Jet comply with a host of special conditions before approval was granted. On July 31, 1964, a mere 10 months after first flight, the Lear Jet was FAA certificated, beating the Jet Commander by several months.

More than 1,800 Learjets have been sold in the 35 years that have passed since the first one took to the air. The reputation of the aircraft and its designer have made Learjet a household word, even among people who never have seen a business jet.

equipment became available for all general aviation aircraft. An increasing number of manufacturers began producing avionics that complied with FAA Technical Standard Orders (TSOs), which set performance and production standards for various classes of airborne equipment.

Major avionics manufacturers—such as Aircraft Radio Corporation (ARC), Bendix, Collins, RCA, Sperry and Wilcox—recognized the potential of the top end of the general aviation market. As early as 1959, Narco, a specialty avionics manufacturer for general aviation, began developing a lightweight DME unit for small aircraft, while King Radio started what would become a complete line of avionics for lighter airplanes. Cessna eventually acquired ARC and developed its own line of avionics for general aviation.

Turbocharged piston-powered airplanes, such as the Cessna 320 Skyknight, came into vogue during the 1960s.

National Air & Space Museum, Smithsonian Institution, Photo No. 97-15892

By the early 1960s, many business aircraft were being outfitted with
dual instrumentation, which quickly filled available instrument panel
space. Smaller, lighter gyros helped ease that problem, replacing the larger
military-surplus units that business aviation had been using for more than
a decade. Many airframe manufacturers began offering optional higher-
powered generators and electrical systems to handle the increased
demands of the plethora of new onboard electronics.

By the mid-1960s, new safety devices, including cockpit voice
recorders (CVRs) and flight data recorders (FDRs), became mandatory in
commercial jetliners, and many leading business-jet operators began
installing CVRs and FDRs as well. Advanced avionics, from more capable
radar and the famous Collins FD-108 flight director to long-range sys-

*L.B. Smith's Tempo II, a pressurized
conversion of the Douglas A-26 that
could carry up to 10 passengers in
air-conditioned comfort, received
FAA certification in late 1960.*

Flying magazine

tems, such as inertial navigation and Loran, were installed on many business jets. In 1966, cockpit technology had advanced to the point where the Jet Commander became the first business aircraft to be approved for lower (Category II) landing minimums.

While some of the largest U.S. corporations moved into turbine-powered aircraft shortly after they were introduced, the business fleet of this era actually was a mix of tried-and-true, large reciprocating-engine transports, along with a variety of piston-powered single- and twin-engine general aviation aircraft and a growing number of new business jets and turboprops.

Surplus World War II military aircraft, such as the Douglas A-26 and Lockheed Ventura, were still being converted to business use, largely

Improved versions of the Beech 18 continued to be manufactured into the 1960s, while modifiers introduced numerous enhancements for earlier models of the popular twin-piston airplane.

National Air & Space Museum, Smithsonian Institution, Photo No. 94-9217

The six-seat Piper Aztec was part of the class of light twin-engine aircraft that became widely used by businesses during the 1960s.

Flying magazine (Nigel Moll)

because these durable machines could fly typical business-aviation missions nearly as high and fast as the new turbine-powered business aircraft. Yet they cost up to one-third less to buy and outfit with state-of-the-art equipment. Dee Howard won acclaim for his conversions of the Ventura, and popular conversions of the A-26 included L.B. Smith's Tempo II and the On Mark Marketeer. Upgraded and converted airliners—such as the Convair 240 and Lockheed Lodestar—were popular too because they offered competitive performance at a relatively low price.

A variety of modification packages for the Beech 18 and DC-3 kept those venerable aircraft productive through the 1960s. One of the most popular improvements to the Beech 18 was Volpar's tricycle landing gear kit, which Beech later installed on new production airplanes. Other modifications of the Beech 18 and DC-3 included re-engining those proven airframes with turboprops.

Several innovative modifiers, such as Jack Riley of Fort Lauderdale and San Antonio's Ed Swearingen, used their talents to improve the speed and efficiency of piston-powered general aviation aircraft. Swearingen streamlined the Twin Bonanza to create the Excalibur, and Riley's Turbo Rocket, a turbocharged version of the Cessna 310, was one of the fastest piston light twins of the era.

With performance-enhancing packages available for many of the existing piston-powered business aircraft, some operators shunned the higher-speed turbine aircraft, preferring to stay with the familiar, less-expensive airplanes. But the days of the large, piston-powered transport were numbered, business aviation's need for performance favored the turbines.

For example, the Rolls-Royce Dart, which powered the Fokker F-27 and Gulfstream I, had an inflight shutdown rate that was markedly better than that of contemporary piston powerplants. In many areas, jet fuel cost less than the aviation gasoline used in piston-powered aircraft and was available at most major airports by the late 1950s. Finally, aircraft

Germany's HFB 320 Hansa Jet, which featured distinctive forward-swept wings, was one of the first-generation business jets, but only a handful of American businesses operated the aircraft.

Flying magazine

marketers, such as Remmert-Werner, guaranteed that the operating costs of their new turbine aircraft would be comparable to or better than those of the Convair, DC-3, Lodestar or similar piston-powered aircraft.

Initially, some companies balked at exchanging a $100,000 military-surplus airplane for a million-dollar business jet, and some older aviators wondered privately if they could handle the fast new aircraft. But the productivity gains possible with turbine-powered transports eventually won over many operators.

The relatively high acquisition cost of the new turbine equipment actually had a beneficial, if originally unanticipated, consequence. Chief

NBAA's Unsung Heroes

As any Chairman or President of NBAA will concede, it is the Staff of the Association that makes it easier for Member Companies to go about their daily business of providing efficient, on-demand air transportation. Two of the longest-serving NBAA staffers who have had a lasting impact on the Association beginning in the 1960s were Frederick B. McIntosh and John A. Pope, both of whom rose to be vice presidents of the organization.

McIntosh, who worked for NBAA from 1964 through 1983, is best remembered for helping craft FAR Part 91 Subpart D. This regulation allowed business aircraft owners to retain operational flexibility in meeting safety goals at a time when the FAA was prepared to enact draconian compliance schemes in the wake of a horrendous 1969 charter aircraft accident. McIntosh also helped develop a truce in the battle between aircraft operators and airport management at noise-sensitive Westchester County Airport in White Plains, New York. These victories, as well as his daily professional liaison with FAA officials, helped elevate NBAA's stature among Washington regulators.

Pope, who served the Association from 1961 through 1984, was responsible for developing the NBAA trade show into a sophisticated, revenue-generating exhibition of the latest business aviation equipment and services. "Pope John" also was instrumental in developing the Association's operations manual template, and he conducted more than 20 workshops in which he helped dozens of flight departments develop standard procedures and policies.

NBAA

NBAA Vice President Frederick B. McIntosh was a key figure in the creation of FAR Part 91 Subpart D, a regulation that gave business aircraft needed operational flexibility.

NBAA

After spending more than 20 years with NBAA, John A. Pope became an aviation consultant and writer.

The North American Aviation Sabreliner, a derivative of the U.S. Air Force T-39, was introduced in 1963. St. Louis-based Pet Milk Company was the first customer to take delivery of the six-passenger, twin-engine business jet.

Sabreliner Corporation

pilots, who formerly were content to merely fly the company aircraft, were now stewards of sophisticated million-dollar assets that had to be justified and carefully managed.

In fact, the changeover from operating piston-powered aircraft to turbine equipment required prudent planning by operators and thorough retraining of pilots and mechanics by major airlines and training specialists such as FlightSafety International. Aviators had to become acquainted with new terms and concepts—such as balanced field length, buffet boundary, foreign object damage and tuck under—and they had to fly strictly by the numbers instead of by the seat of their pants. The FAA suggested that business aircraft pilots undergo formal transition training, and the agency soon required that aviators be retrained bi-annually in their specific model of aircraft.

The larger financial commitment and technical expertise needed to operate turbine aircraft led a growing number of companies to examine alternatives to buying and operating airplanes. Some firms hired experienced operators to fly and manage their aircraft; other companies leased or chartered aircraft.

Executive Jet Aviation (EJA) of Columbus, Ohio, one of the largest operators offering business jet service on a contract basis, was founded during this era. By positioning its fleet of Learjets at strategic locations around the country, EJA was able to eliminate charges for ferry time and deadhead trips (journeys with no revenue-paying passengers) and could offer competitively priced, on-demand air service.

Those companies that chose the traditional approach of establishing in-house flight departments received operational support from NBAA. One of the Association's most important contributions was the *Guide to Management Policies for Business Aircraft,* which was distributed for the first time at its 10th Annual Meeting in Denver in October 1957. The proto-type operations manual—which was written by Harley D. Kysor, an air-line pilot, aviation consultant and contributing editor to *Business & Commercial Aviation* magazine—served as a guide to good operating prac-tices for aviation departments. Beginning in the late 1960s, NBAA also conducted annual salary surveys of flight department personnel to help managers determine the going rates for compensation and to develop a data base on industry employment practices.

As the fleet of business and commercial jets mushroomed in the 1960s, an unwanted byproduct was noise. As early as the late 1950s, com-

JBT Associates

By launching the sales programs of three landmark business jets—the Dassault Falcon, Cessna Citation and Canadair Challenger—James B. Taylor helped define and refine the art of marketing business jets.

AvData & Weekly of Business Aviation

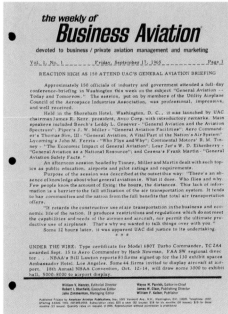

John Zimmerman, president of Wichita-based Aviation Data Service, helped launch the Weekly of Business Aviation, *a newsletter that has been published in Washington, D.C. since 1965.*

munities near airports, especially in New York and Southern California, began pressing for curfews and other operational restrictions on turbojet-powered aircraft. Eventually, the FAA realized that noise was a national, not a local, problem, and the agency moved to require anti-noise zoning at federally funded airports. The development of quieter, new-generation turbofans, such as the Pratt & Whitney JT15D, also helped lower the decibel level. NBAA did its part by encouraging Members to adopt noise-abatement procedures. However, noise was a problem that would continue to hamper the industry.

Another unfortunate result of the rapid growth of business and commercial flying in the 1960s was airport and airways congestion. Despite the best efforts of the FAA, aviation system capacity lagged. As delays mounted, tensions between business aviation and airlines rose, as each group sought unimpeded access to airports and airspace.

Various solutions to the problem were offered. However, as congestion at major airfields grew, air carriers, which had previously encouraged business aircraft passengers to connect with commercial flights, suggested

Left: Professional Pilot *magazine, which debuted in 1967, is noted for its reader surveys. For example, each year the publication takes a poll to determine the best business aviation FBOs.*

Right: Murray Q. Smith, *founder of* Professional Pilot *magazine, has served as its publisher for the past 30 years.*

©1997 Robert B. Parke

excluding general aviation from the busiest terminals. Several midair collisions involving airliners and general aviation aircraft exacerbated the animosity. Air traffic controllers also felt the pressure of trying to cope with the large volume of air traffic, regarless of its source, and their frustrations would lead to slowdowns and strikes in the years to come.

Interestingly, it was a two-month-long airline strike during the summer of 1966 that underscored how important business aviation was to the national transportation system. When machinists at five trunk airlines walked out on July 8, travelers were forced to find alternative transportation. Throughout the 43-day job action, general aviation movements set records at major airports, such as Washington National and New York's LaGuardia Airport, and air taxi revenues jumped 20 percent or more.

Believing that the ultimate solution to the country's transportation problems was to coordinate regulation of transportation, a restructured FAA—the Federal Aviation Administration—was one of several organizations that were made part of the newly created Department of Transportation (DOT), which was formed in April 1967. Business aviation was about to enter a new and challenging era.

The Bristol Siddeley exhibit was typical of the booths that were set up at Los Angeles' Ambassador Hotel during the 1965 NBAA Convention. This display is quite modest compared to the large, high-tech presentations of major aviation manufacturers at contemporary NBAA Shows.

Scott E. Miller

CHAPTER 5

Growing Sophistication

By the late 1960s, mankind was flying to new heights. In 1969 alone, the world witnessed the maiden flights of a new commercial supersonic transport and the first wide-body airliner and watched on television as Neil Armstrong became the first man to set foot on the moon.

Business aviation also continued to fly high at the end of the decade. Many companies and individual businessmen, impressed with the growing capability of new general aviation aircraft, began flying for the first time. Existing operators stepped up into larger, faster and longer-range aircraft, such as the new turbofan-powered Gulfstream II. Others added more aircraft to their fleets, including new types, such as the emerging class of twin turbine-powered helicopters.

But while the horizons of flight were expanding, the social changes that were sweeping America had a direct impact on business aviation.

Gulfstream Aerospace

The turbofan-powered Gulfstream II opened a new era in long-range company flying in 1968, when the aircraft became the first business jet to make a nonstop transatlantic crossing from the United States.

Ted Smith's Aerostar light twin was noted for its speed and graceful shape. Piper later assumed responsibility for manufacturing the airplane.

Organizations representing black and female pilots urged flight departments to end what they perceived were discriminatory hiring practices. Corporations became targets of "anti-establishment" demonstrators and received bomb threats, some directed at their aircraft. As Cuba became a favorite destination of airline hijackers, businesses worried that their aircraft might be commandeered, too. Security guards were hired to watch company airplanes, aircraft alarm systems were developed and fences were erected around many hangars to thwart sabotage and other possible attacks.

Although few business aircraft operators were victimized by terrorist tactics, virtually everyone was affected by the growing congestion and resulting delays in the air traffic control (ATC) system. Beginning in the summer of 1968, the problem was dramatized and exacerbated by a series of air traffic controller slowdowns in which aircraft were handled "by the book."

Various solutions to congestion were proposed, from banning or discouraging general aviation at busy terminals to "de-peaking" airline schedules. In 1969, the FAA imposed a temporary reservations system for opera-

Edward J. Swearingen, a longtime modifier of aircraft, also built a number of new airplanes, including the turboprop-powered, pressurized Merlin II.

In 1974, Beech launched a pressurized version of the Baron, a popular twin-engine aircraft designed for the businessman-pilot.

Flying magazine

tors conducting instrument flights at five of the busiest fields: Washington National, Chicago O'Hare and at Kennedy, LaGuardia and Newark airports serving New York City. One-hour landing and takeoff slots at each field were rationed by a central office in Washington under what became known as the "high-density rule."

The "temporary" restrictions, which were still in place in 1997, eased congestion somewhat, but everyone knew that the long-term solution to overcrowding was to increase ATC system capacity. Political and economic realities dictated that operators would have to pay part of the price to upgrade the air transportation network.

Cost allocation studies were performed to determine how the expenses would be divided among the airlines, general aviation and the federal government, which, because of the military, was itself an ATC system user. The end result was a series of levies on airline tickets, air freight shipments, international airline departures and general aviation fuels. Beginning in 1970, the revenue was deposited into a "trust fund" that was earmarked to finance capital improvements to airports and airways.

Unfortunately, the ink on the Airport and Airway Development Act of 1970 was barely dry before money was diverted for other purposes.

E.E. "Dunny" Dunsworth was a World War II Marine Corps pilot before organizing the Trunkline Gas Company flight department in 1950. Thirty-five years later, he retired as head of the department. He was an NBAA Director from 1964 to 1973 and served as the Association's President from 1969 to 1971.

NBAA

While funds were spent on worthwhile infrastructure improvement projects, including the construction of "reliever" airports that general aviation aircraft can use instead of major terminals, billions of supposedly dedicated monies have been used to offset the federal budget deficit or pay for FAA operations. Despite the shortcomings of this financing approach, business aviation, over the years, has reluctantly agreed to continue the same basic ATC system funding concept adopted in 1970.

Part of the challenge of expanding the ATC system has been not to merely build more airports, but to redesign the airspace according to a master plan that increases utilization of airways and airports while maximizing safety. Perhaps the key change in airspace design during the 1970s was the establishment of terminal control areas (TCAs), inverted wedding cake-

Southern California has long been a hotbed of business flying, and Van Nuys Airport is a favorite destination of Los Angeles-bound business people.

©1997 Paul Brou

shaped zones of positive control located around major U.S. airports.

Other ATC changes instituted during this era included mandatory use of encoding altimeters (which helped controllers better track and monitor air traffic), development of area navigation (RNAV) routings and approaches, establishment of a speed limit for all aircraft operating under 10,000 feet (which made it easier for pilots to "see and avoid" high-performance aircraft), and expansion of the number of runways qualified for lower (Category II) approach minimums.

Although a practical collision avoidance system still was beyond aviation's reach, improved ground-based ATC equipment was installed nationwide. Also, work began on the microwave landing system, which offered potential advantages over the standard instrument landing system (ILS).

Two strong supporters of business aviation have been Edward W. Stimpson (left), longtime President of the General Aviation Manufacturers Association (GAMA) and Cessna CEO Russell W. Meyer, Jr. (right), who has been Chairman of GAMA three times since the organization was founded in 1970.

John Winant, Mr. NBAA

Virtually anyone who has been associated with NBAA will tell you that no one has had a more pervasive personal impact on the Association than John H. Winant.

A combat-decorated Marine Corps infantry officer in World War II, Winant first got involved in business aviation in 1957 when he became director of industrial relations and director of aviation for the Sprague Electric Company of North Adams, Massachusetts. During the same year, he was elected to NBAA's Board of Directors and served in all of the Association's volunteer elected-officer positions until he was named President of the group (equivalent to the Chairman's job today), a post he held from 1961 to 1964. Finally, in 1971, Winant accepted NBAA's offer to go to Washington, D.C. and head the Association's headquarters Staff.

Winant was tested immediately by a series of crises, such as the federal government's proposed 40-percent reduction in fuel allocated to business aviation as a result of the oil embargo. Still, he was able to build confidence in NBAA as "an Association with purpose," more than triple membership, forge a "credible link" between NBAA and other Washington, D.C.-based industry and government groups and enhance NBAA's image and effectiveness with Congress. It was in Washington's backroom bargaining sessions that Winant excelled; his firm yet gentleman-like negotiating prowess earned him the respect of proponents and opponents alike.

Besides leading NBAA from 1971 to 1986, Winant helped shape the NASA-operated Aviation Safety Reporting System (ASRS), which provides aviation system users with a means of reporting safety deficiencies confidentially. He also was instrumental in the formation of the International Business Aviation Council (IBAC), a federation of national and regional business aviation associations. Another of his lasting contributions was *Keep Business Flying*, a book that documented the growth of NBAA through its first 40 years.

Restructuring NBAA to Meet the Challenges of the 1970s

During the 1972 NBAA Convention, Mrs. William K. Lawton, widow of the NBAA's Executive Director from 1956 to 1966, presented a 25th Anniversary plaque to NBAA Chairman John B. Bean (second from right) as President John H. Winant (right) and Vice President John A. Pope (left) looked on.

John B. Bean, a World War II Naval aviator and pilot-executive with International Milling Corporation, recognized soon after he joined the NBAA Board of Directors in 1968 that the Association's Staff needed to be restructured in order to deal effectively with the mounting problems facing business aircraft operators. Bean helped reorganize NBAA and search for an experienced, full-time chief of staff. The appointment of John Winant as NBAA President in 1971 assured strong internal leadership and excellent representation in Washington.

During his term as NBAA Chairman from 1971 to 1973, Bean also devoted his energies to making certain that FAA officials understood the performance capabilities of modern business aircraft so that they would not be routinely delayed at some airports because air traffic controllers believed business aircraft couldn't maintain high enough approach speeds to keep up with airliners.

As threats to the operational freedom of business and other general aviation aircraft multiplied by the early 1970s, a move to unite general aviation organizations was launched. While the effort was well-intentioned and helped establish a common front on some issues, Bean said the movement foundered because of unreconcilable differences among some of the groups.

Bean remained on the NBAA Board until 1976. He served the Association during a turbulent time, but it was also one that established a stronger and more efficient Staff to serve the needs of a membership that was itself growing in stature.

Likewise, new technologies and procedures were applied to the nagging problem of aircraft noise. However, the continuing growth of jet traffic, coupled with inappropriate development of land near airports, increased the pressure to institute bans, curfews or otherwise limit flight activity at many airports important to business aviation, such as those in Burbank and Santa Monica, California; Morristown, New Jersey; Westchester County, New York and Washington, D.C.

Despite installation of sound-suppressing equipment on aircraft, adoption of noise-abatement flying techniques and enactment of new federal rules (FAR Part 36) limiting the amount of noise that aircraft engines could emit, tensions between aircraft operators and residents who lived near airports mounted.

The harshest critics of aircraft noise lobbied to have the U.S. Environmental Protection Agency (EPA) assume responsibility for regulating aircraft emissions. However, by the late 1970s, the FAA had reasserted its authority to establish and administer aircraft noise rules on a national basis, which would be an important principle in the many lawsuits that would arise.

A shorter-term, yet nearly fatal blow was dealt to business aviation in

Flying magazine

Dwane L. Wallace (right), Chairman of the Board, and Del Roskam, President, led Cessna during its halcyon days.

Oil companies, traditionally one of the biggest users of company aircraft, have made Houston's Hobby Airport a center of business flying for many years.

©1997 Paul Brou

1973, when an oil embargo triggered government restrictions on the availability of aviation fuel in the United States. A mandatory fuel allocation program was imposed by the federal government in November, and initially business aviation was targeted for a 40-percent cut.

Within six weeks, the situation eased and business aviation users suffered only a 10-percent reduction. NBAA, which was instrumental in getting the business aviation allocation increased, established a round-the-clock information center to help aircraft operators determine the availability of fuel at the airports they planned to visit. The Association, with the approval of the federal government and the cooperation of nearly 1,000 fuel vendors, also organized a fuel reservation program to ensure that aircraft operators had enough aviation gasoline or jet fuel to complete essential trips.

The Citation 500 was the first of Cessna's light business jets. The twin turbofan-powered airplane proved popular because of its short-field capabilities and docile handling characteristics.

The fuel crisis taught business aircraft operators an important lesson: From now on they would need to fly more efficiently, not only to save money and conserve resources but to minimize adverse effects on the environment. Flight departments began practicing a number of fuel-saving fly-

Cessna Aircraft

By 1968, Beech had added the new Bonanza 36 to its product line. The six-seat aircraft proved popular among air taxi operators.

Business & Commercial Aviation magazine

ing techniques, such as using long-range cruise settings and carrying only the amount of fuel needed for the trip, rather than topping off the tanks and operating at heavier, less-efficient weights.

Aviation department managers also audited their operations to find ways to enhance efficiency and productivity. Part of the solution was to uti-

Active on Many Fronts

"It was our intention [at NBAA] to take a position on all important questions," declared William F. Gilbert, who was Weyerhaeuser's aviation manager when he joined the NBAA Board of Directors in 1970. "That way, we could make our presence known and gain some recognition.

"At that time, there were quite a few important things going on," explained Gilbert, who led several NBAA committees and was Chairman of the Association from 1975 to 1977. Among the most ominous were the steps being taken to curtail business aviation's access to major airports. Also, a cost allocation study proposed massive increases in general aviation charges, and NBAA took the lead in opposing them. In addition, several airports were calling for curfews.

"The bottom line was that NBAA had to become involved in lawsuits [to block the curfews] in which the ultimate cost could not be easily judged. Fortunately, we had the determination to go ahead and fight for our rights," said Gilbert.

William F. Gilbert

Since retiring as manager of Weyerhaeuser's flight department in 1985, former NBAA Chairman William F. Gilbert has been involved in activities at Seattle's Museum of Flight.

Learjet

The turbofan-powered Learjet 35 became a mainstay of the business jet fleet during the 1970s.

lize new computerized flight planning and maintenance services to help organize and streamline recordkeeping. Simulators, flight training devices, audio-visual systems and other programs also made training easier.

Chief pilots who had been caught in the economic downdraft of the late 1960s and early 1970s were familiar with the consequences of not managing their assets in a cost-effective manner. During recessions, aviation departments had become prime targets of corporate cost-cutters. Some operators pulled out of aviation altogether; others reduced the size of their fleets. Many postponed new equipment buys.

Some companies that retained their aviation departments during the business dips of the 1970s obtained air taxi and commercial operator (ATCO) certificates so they could charter out their airplanes and thereby generate revenue to offset the fixed costs of flying. Relaxation of Civil Aeronautics Board (CAB) rules regarding the size and type of aircraft that

©1997 Mike Vines

The Citation II, which first flew in 1977, had uprated engines and a longer fuselage and wing than Cessna's original business jet.

could be used in commercial operations made it easier to do. Other companies responded to hard times by disposing of their aircraft and turning to leading charter and management companies, such as Teterboro-based Executive Air Fleet.

Regardless of the avenue by which companies used business aviation, operators had an ever-expanding array of aircraft from which to choose in the late 1960s and early 1970s. Although production of two popular models—the Beech 18 and Gulfstream G-159—ended in 1968, a host of new aircraft were poised to take their place, from Ted Smith's Aerostar piston twin, the stretched Beech King Air 100 and Cessna's new Fanjet 500 (later known as the Citation) to the transcontinental Grumman Gulfstream II business jet and corporate versions of the Boeing 737 and Douglas DC-9. Several manufacturers, undoubtedly encouraged by the progress of the Concorde, were even contemplating development of a supersonic business jet.

This instrument panel of this North American Aviation Sabreliner 60, which featured avionics by Collins, was configured like many of the other business jets of the late 1960s and early 1970s.

Rockwell Collins

The Gulfstream II, which was powered by Rolls-Royce Spey turbofans, was the new flagship of the business aviation fleet. National Distillers and Chemical Corporation took delivery of the first G-II in December 1967. After being outfitted by AiResearch Aviation's Long Island facility, the aircraft flew from Teterboro, New Jersey to London's Gatwick Airport

AiResearch Aviation extended the useful life of the Lockheed JetStar by re-engining the turbojet-powered business jet with Garrett TFE 731 turbofans.

Business & Commercial Aviation magazine

in May 1968, making it the first business jet to fly across the Atlantic non-stop from the United States.

In the mid-1970s, when the larger Gulfstream III was poised to succeed the G-II as the leading top-of-the-line business jet, two competitors emerged. Dassault offered the three-engine Falcon 50, and Canadair took William P. Lear's Lear Star 600 design and developed the first wide-body business jet, aptly called the Challenger.

Besides the introduction of the G-II, the other significant aircraft development of the late 1960s was the announcement of Cessna's first business jet, the Citation, an eight-seat light jet that was powered by two Pratt & Whitney JT15D turbofans. Noting the success of the Beech King Air, Cessna designed the aircraft so that it had good short-field performance and was easy to fly. Priced at $600,000, the company sold Citations direct from the factory, instead of through dealers. The Citation first flew in

Once the government committed to developing the necessary infrastructure for air-to-ground telephones, business aircraft operators began buying airborne equipment, such as the famous Wulfsberg Flitefone. AlliedSignal

©1997 Mike Vines

The popularity of light business jets in the late 1960s and early 1970s led France's Dassault-Breguet to develop the Falcon 10, which, like many of the new business jets of the era, was powered by Garrett TFE 731 turbofans.

Among the most successful of the single-turbine helicopters were the Bell 206 JetRanger and the stretched 206L LongRanger, which first flew in 1974.

September 1969 and was FAA certificated two years later. Within five years, the light jet proved so successful that Cessna expanded the line to include the Citation I, II and III. In 1977, a specially equipped version of the Citation I, called the SP, became the first business jet to receive single-pilot certification.

Meanwhile, most other business jet manufacturers upgraded their aircraft by re-engining them with quieter, cleaner turbofans, especially the Garrett TFE 731, which featured electronic fuel controls that permitted more precise, efficient operations and protected the powerplant from exceeding critical temperatures, pressures and speeds. The Hawker Siddeley H.S. 125-700, Israel Aircraft Industries Westwind (a new version of the Jet Commander), Learjet 35/36, Dassault Falcon 10 and Rockwell Sabreliner 65 all used Garrett TFE 731s. Even the venerable JetStar got a new lease on life by using TFE 731s. Garrett launched the 731 JetStar to convert older JetStars, and Lockheed produced a new aircraft designated the JetStar II.

RONSON AVIATION

Flying magazine. Photo by Nigel Moll

Italy's Agusta 109 was one of the new, light twin-turbine helicopters introduced in the 1970s, and business aircraft operators began to incorporate these new rotorcraft into their fixed-wing fleets.

The single-turbine Hughes 500, a design originally developed for the U.S. Army, proved useful to businesses that needed transportation to remote areas, such as construction sites.

Other derivatives of first-generation business jets emerged. From the highly successful Falcon 20, Dassault developed the smaller Falcon 10 and larger, three-engine Falcon 50, both powered by the TFE 731 turbofan engine. Learjet stretched its basic design into the transcontinental Model 35/36. Meanwhile, Dee Howard and The Raisbeck Group developed performance improvements that kept early-model Learjets competitive.

Beech introduced new and improved versions of the King Air at regular intervals during the 1970s, the most notable of the era being the T-tail Super King Air 200. Rockwell, Piper and Cessna entered the turboprop market as well, offering the Commander 690, Cheyenne and Model 441, respectively. In 1977, even William P. Lear announced he was working on a twin-turboprop aircraft design, although he would not live long enough to see his radical Lear Fan fly.

The popularity of pressurized piston twins also increased during this period. By 1974, nearly 30 percent of the 1,100-unit NBAA fleet was composed of single-aircraft operators of piston twins or light turboprops.

Featuring a T-tail, more powerful engines and a stretched fuselage, the Super King Air 200 became one of the most popular models of the Beech turboprop.

In the helicopter market, Bell built upon the success of its JetRanger by introducing a stretched model called the LongRanger. The trend, however, was toward twin-turbine machines with interiors geared for executive transport and instrument flying capabilities. (Instrument flying in helicopters was pioneered by the Aerospatiale Gazelle.) By the mid-1970s, a new class of light twin rotorcraft emerged. Included in this group were the Agusta 109 and MBB BO-105. By the end of the decade, new, sophisticated helicopters, such as the Bell 222 and Sikorsky S-76, were available. Slowly, operators of fixed-wing aircraft began integrating these more capable rotorcraft into their fleets.

Advances in avionics kept coming, and sophisticated systems were installed in progressively smaller aircraft, especially after the FAA defined

AlliedSignal

King Radio's first solid-state navigation/communications unit was the KX-170, which was introduced in 1969.

Remembering the Fuel Crisis

NBAA

Midcoast Aviation's John Tucker

In 1973, John Tucker, President and CEO of NBAA Associate Member Midcoast Aviation, had one very big matter on his mind. His company, along with other FBOs,

was operating under fuel price controls that had been instituted in response to the oil embargo.

"I give full credit to NBAA for having those restraints lifted, even though it might have seemed to be...detrimental to the best interests of their Regular [aircraft operating] Members," said Tucker.

Business aircraft operators expected to buy fuel at the lowest practical price. But if FBOs had lost too much money selling fuel at the artificially low controlled prices and consequently went out of business, the entire industry would have suffered.

"Although other organizations had appealed to Congress for relief on our behalf, nothing happened," said Tucker. "But when [NBAA President] John Winant spoke to the appropriate Congressional committees, they listened and soon the problem was solved." It was a good example of how aircraft operators and FBOs could work together for the good of the industry, said Tucker.

It also was a good example of how Tucker's leadership and unique experience in business aviation allowed him to adopt a balanced position. Before joining Midcoast, he had been President of the Butler Aviation FBO chain. Earlier, he was Executive Vice President of Remmert-Werner, the St. Louis business aircraft sales organization.

Part of the challenge of expanding the ATC system has been not to merely build more airports, but to redesign the airspace according to a master plan that increases utilization of airways and airports while maximizing safety.

Naturally, airframe manufacturers were among the biggest users of business aircraft. Beech executives, including Executive Vice President Frank E. Hedrick (left) and King Air Program Manager T.W. Gillespie (second from left), boarded a King Air for a business trip in June 1964.

Business & Commercial Aviation magazine

minimum operational performance characteristics for all general aviation avionics gear used in the ATC system.

The 1970s saw the emergence of integrated avionics packages, digital and color weather radar (with flat plate antennae), area navigation (RNAV) equipment, airborne telephones, emergency locator transmitters (ELTs) and 360-channel very high frequency (VHF) communications radios. Use of horizontal situation indicators (HSIs) also became popular.

The Cessna 340 was one of a class of piston-powered, pressurized twins that was flown by businessmen-pilots in the 1970s.

Cessna Aircraft

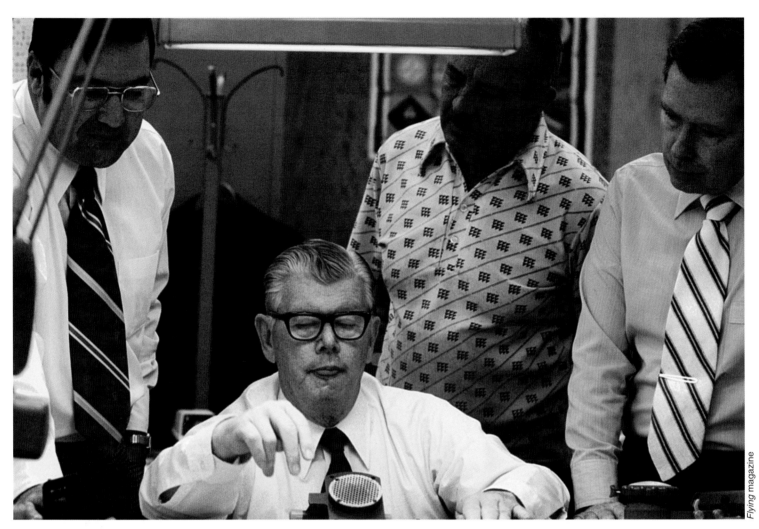

Flying magazine

William P. Lear continued to develop new aircraft designs after he sold Lear Jet Industries. During the 1970s, he came up with the Lear Star 600 (which was reshaped into the Canadair Challenger) and the turboprop-powered Lear Fan.

High frequency (HF) communications radios and long-range navigation systems—inertial navigation, Omega and very low frequency (VLF)—became increasingly important to business aircraft operators operating overseas, especially those flying across the North Atlantic at preferred cruising altitudes, in airspace where long-range navigation equipment was required beginning in 1977.

The growing sophistication of business flying required professionally trained pilots and managers. Starting in the mid-1970s, leading institutions of higher learning, such as Embry-Riddle Aeronautical University, established college-level courses designed to prepare students for careers in business aviation. The FAA instituted more-stringent requirements for recurrent training of pilots of turbine-powered aircraft, and more business aviators utilized simulators to meet those higher training standards.

Collins

Collins pioneered the development of electronic flight instrument systems (EFIS) for business aircraft in the mid-1980s. The company's EFIS 84 system was featured in the cockpit of the Dassault Falcon 100.

During this era, the Cessna Caravan became the first of the single-engine turboprop aircraft to enter wide-scale service. Williams International introduced the FJ44, a small turbofan engine that would soon power a new class of small business jets. Also, the FAA and NASA began to study the viability of a civil tilt rotor, a new type of aircraft that could take off and land like a helicopter yet cruise as fast as an airplane. Other technical advances were applied to business aircraft, some for the first time anywhere in aviation. An increasing number of aircraft components were fabricated from composites to save weight (and thus fuel), and winglets were installed on business jets and turboprops to improve their cruise performance.

While orders for new business aircraft languished, used aircraft sales remained robust, and the market for avionics and specialized aviation support services—such as flight planning, computerized recordkeeping and real-time weather reports—flourished.

New products introduced during the late 1970s and early 1980s included the Ryan Stormscope, a new type of weather avoidance device that

James Holahan, Aviation Editor

James Holahan, a co-founder of Aviation International News, has been Editor-in-Chief for more than 25 years.

Aviation International News, business aviation's tabloid-size publication, was first published in 1972 at the NBAA Annual Meeting & Convention in Cincinnati.

It's little wonder that James Holahan won NBAA's 1996 Platinum Wing Award for lifetime achievement in aviation journalism. Not only did he serve for eight years as Editor-in-Chief of one of the industry's premier magazines, *Business & Commercial Aviation*, in 1972, he and Wilson Leach co-founded a tabloid-sized convention newspaper that has evolved into *Aviation International News*, a leading source of information on business aviation.

Originally called *NBAA Convention News* and first distributed at the Association's 1972 Annual Meeting in Cincinnati, by 1977 the publication was being published at the Reading Air Show in

Pennsylvania and at the annual Helicopter Association International meetings. These editions, when combined with pre- and post-show issues, grew to be the bimonthly periodical known as *Aviation Convention News*. Eventually, it was renamed *Aviation International News* and is now published monthly, along with several special convention issues.

During this entire time, James Holahan has been the driving force behind the publication's excellent editorial product, drawing upon his experience as a military aviator, radio engineer and commercial pilot to provide a unique perspective on the community.

With the need to attract qualified candidates to fill increasingly complex flight department jobs, compensation became an important subject for managers and pilots alike and led to the development of numerous salary surveys. In addition, larger flight department budgets prompted some companies to insist that their chief pilots undergo management training. Other firms installed non-flying leaders with extensive management experience to ensure that their aviation assets were properly administered.

NBAA became more of an important resource for business aircraft operators during this era, and one of the Association's greatest achievements of the 1970s was to help shape a complex federal regulation known as FAR Part 91 Subpart D.

In an effort to plug a loophole in existing rules that allowed unqualified operators to fly charters, the FAA wanted to amend and extend the definition of commercial operator in a way that NBAA said "could largely discourage the use of aircraft in most corporate operations."

The Hostess of New Orleans

Janice K. Barden's company, Aviation Personnel International, has been an NBAA Member for years, but Barden is best known as the local chairperson of the five NBAA Conventions that have been held in New Orleans. She hopes to be appointed to do the job again in the year 2000.

Barden was an industrial psychologist who, at the urging of several of her associates in aviation, set up shop in the late 1950s at New Jersey's Teterboro Airport, a center of business flying. Her objective was to devise a battery of psychological and other tests to help determine what type of person would most likely be successful in aviation. By the time Barden attended her first NBAA Convention in Denver in 1957, she had relocated to New Orleans and had attracted a number of business aviation clients.

Since then, Barden's personnel placement and testing business has thrived, and her understanding of business aviation personnel requirements is constantly being fine tuned as the industry evolves. While Barden's professional services have been used occasionally by NBAA, it is her vitality, enthusiasm and organizational skills that have endeared her not only to the Convention planning group, but to virtually everyone in the Association.

Janice K. Barden

Fortunately, NBAA's Frederick B. McIntosh helped the FAA revise its original proposal, which allowed business aircraft owners to retain their traditional operational flexibility, yet defined the parameters for time-sharing and interchange agreements, transporting sales prospects, conducting aircraft sales demonstrations, carrying cargo and other types of business flying missions. The final rule also established a set of defined maintenance programs.

Business aviation also faced a host of other regulatory issues by the late 1970s. NBAA and a sister organization, the General Aviation Manufacturers Association (GAMA), worked together on a number of problems, including resisting Internal Revenue Service attempts to tax certain types of business aircraft use by company employees.

GAMA and NBAA also began what would be a long and arduous campaign against the huge product liability judgments against aircraft manufacturers—damage awards that ultimately would increase the cost and stifle development of new business aircraft.

From the early 1950s through the early 1980s, the Reading Maintenance and Operations Meeting was probably the second most important show for business aviation, next to the NBAA Convention. The exhibition, which was held each year in eastern Pennsylvania, included a contest among business aircraft, with the top award going to the aircraft that was judged to be the "Flagship of the Industrial Fleet."

Business & Commercial Aviation magazine

CHAPTER 6

New Horizons for Business Flying

Beginning in 1978, business aviation suffered through one of the most turbulent eras in its history. Deregulation of the U.S. airline industry—and the resulting explosive growth of new, low-cost commercial air carriers—strained the air traffic control (ATC) system. It also heightened tensions between airlines and general aviation, as each sought unfettered access to airports large and small. Jetliner service became concentrated on already heavily traveled routes. Turboprop-powered commuter and regional aircraft carried passengers from smaller communities to major airports so they could connect with long-range flights as part of the emerging hub-and-spoke network of commercial air service.

In time, fewer nonstop commercial flights between all but the largest U.S. cities would create more demand for the direct, efficient service provided by business aircraft. However, the initial years following airline deregulation did not produce a windfall for business flying. In fact, as more people traveled by airline and the airspace became more congested, public support for restrictions on business aviation increased.

Perhaps fittingly, 1978 was the high water mark in annual deliveries of new general aviation aircraft. American factories churned out nearly 18,000 units that year, and shipments of business jets peaked in 1981. But the double-digit inflation of the late 1970s, the recession of the early 1980s, rising operating costs and a wave of corporate mergers and acquisitions during this period stifled demand for new aircraft for the rest of the decade.

However, the greatest challenge to business aviation during this era was the 1981 air traffic controllers strike. When 13,000 of the country's

Dassault Falcon Jet. Photo by Bud Davisson.

The three-engine Dassault Falcon 50 was one of a class of "heavy iron" business jets that emerged in the 1970s.

After most of the air traffic controllers went on strike in August 1981, NBAA staffers manned phones round-the-clock to give aircraft operators the latest information concerning delays in the ATC system.

17,000 controllers left their radar scopes on August 3 and refused to return, President Ronald Reagan made good on his threat to terminate the government workers.

The FAA considered banning all but scheduled airline flights to prevent the ATC system from disintegrating. Fortunately, NBAA and other aviation groups quickly convinced FAA Administrator J. Lynn Helms that general aviation aircraft could also fly safely within the system if sensible emergency procedures were instituted.

For the first 72 hours after the walkout, business aircraft operators were asked to conduct only essential flights, and some who flew during the first days of the strike actually were denied ATC services. Subsequently, flow control procedures and a general aviation reservation (GAR) system were established to meter air traffic. Aircraft were held on the ground until it was relatively certain that they could proceed to their destination without inordinate delay.

The diversity of the business aviation industry has always been reflected in the NBAA Convention's static aircraft display, which each year gives operators a chance to inspect the latest equipment.

Business & Commercial Aviation magazine

Flying magazine. Photo by Nigel Moll.

NBAA established a 24-hour toll-free hotline that business aircraft operators called to get the latest air traffic reports. More than three years later, with the ATC system still feeling the aftereffects of the strike, the Association established the FASST (fly around saturated sectors and terminals) service, which provided information on what to expect each day concerning flow control, including the latest list of "red sectors" (congested areas).

More than ever, the federal government needed a master plan for expanding aviation system capacity. In 1982, FAA Administrator Helms announced the National Airspace System Plan (NASP), the blueprint for a sweeping overhaul of the ATC system. The NASP—which defined the research and development, as well as the facilities and equipment needed through the year 2000—continued to rely on ground-based air traffic control techniques, but it called for consolidation of facilities, mainly through

Piper began producing turboprop-powered business aircraft in the early 1970s. The Cheyenne IIXL, which was introduced in 1981, featured a longer fuselage and more powerful engines than previous versions of the Cheyenne II.

©1997 Paul Bowen

The Citation III differed markedly from earlier versions of the Cessna business jet. The aircraft, which was introduced in the late 1970s, featured a swept supercritical wing, stretched fuselage, T-tail and more powerful Garrett TFE 731 engines.

use of computers and automation. For example, many local flight service stations and weather observation stations were to be replaced by a number of automated regional facilities.

Business aircraft operators were given the opportunity to provide input for the new ATC system design through their participation in the National Airspace Review. Thirty NBAA Member Companies, following the example of H.B. Zachry Company's Byron M. "Skip" Reed, volunteered to participate in the 42-month-long exercise.

Although a long-term solution to the ATC system's chronic shortcomings appeared to be in the offing, near-term prospects for improvement were not as rosy. The law that provided funding for capital improvements to the airports and airways had expired in 1979 and was not renewed until 1982. Worse yet, the trust fund had a growing balance because much of the money was being used to offset the federal budget deficit instead of being used to build and upgrade airports and ATC facilities.

Air traffic increased as the United States emerged from the recession of the early 1980s, putting added pressure on the country's aviation infrastructure. Radical solutions to airport and airways congestion—such as privatizing the ATC system or buying and selling landing and takeoff slots to the highest bidder—were proposed and rejected. Unfortunately, progress on more practical concepts, such as joint use of military airports by civil aircraft, was slow.

Besides the system-wide problem of lagging ATC capacity, business aviation was facing several local problems that had national implications. The number of airports with curfew and other noise-based operating restrictions rose so rapidly through the 1980s that NBAA started publishing an annual compendium of the operating rules for hundreds of noise-sensitive airfields across the United States. And when airport authorities became too aggressive in their attempts to mitigate noise, NBAA felt compelled to defend aircraft operators' rights to operate without unreasonable restrictions.

The primary aircraft-noise battleground during the 1980s was Santa Monica, California. The airport, which was a key Los Angeles area general aviation facility, was hemmed in on all four sides by homes and apartments. After jet operations began there in the 1960s, local residents began suing the city for alleged damages caused by aircraft noise. Finally, the airport instituted stringent operating restrictions, including a ban on all jet operations.

©1997 Paul Brou

NBAA

Left: This is the distinctive tower at a popular California business destination, Santa Monica Municipal Airport, which was known as Clover Field when Douglas Aircraft established a major facility there in the 1920s.

Right: Curfews and other operating restrictions jumped dramatically at U.S. airports during the 1970s and 1980s in response to the increasing use of business and commercial jets. A major legal battle pitted aircraft operators against local residents of Santa Monica, California, where a ban on jet operations was enacted, challenged in court and eventually overturned.

109

Business & Commercial Aviation magazine

Top: The emergence of state-of-the-art, twin-turbine helicopters, such as the Bell 222, led to greater use of rotary wing aircraft for business flying.

Bottom: Westchester County Airport, situated less than an hour's drive north of New York City, has been a center of business flying for many years. Because of its location in the midst of affluent suburbs, the airport is one of the most noise-sensitive in the United States.

Flying magazine. Photo by Nigel Moll.

In August 1978, NBAA and GAMA initiated legal action to overturn Santa Monica's jet ban, and a year later it was ruled discriminatory and unconstitutional. However, other operating restrictions were allowed to remain in place. Subsequently, the city tried to effectively ban business jets by establishing noise thresholds that were so low it would preclude their operation. Five years after the initial legal action, the case was finally resolved and business jets were allowed to fly into and out of Santa Monica.

Meanwhile, another vexing noise situation was festering on the East Coast. Westchester County Airport, a center of business aviation activity located in the suburbs of New York City, had been experiencing noise complaints since the mid-1970s. Despite a series of agreements designed to accommodate both the needs of local residents and aircraft operators, NBAA finally had to sue to overturn a mandatory curfew at the airfield. Eventually, the airport, surrounding communities and aircraft operators agreed on a voluntary curfew as a compromise solution.

Other local issues of importance to business aviation during this era included the Port Authority of New York & New Jersey's attempts to restrict general aviation at the major New York city airports. In addition, airspace conflicts between airliners using New Jersey's Newark Airport and business aircraft flying out of nearby Teterboro Airport plagued operators until the issue was finally resolved in 1987, in large part due to NBAA's efforts.

As flight departments struggled to operate in the constricted ATC system of the early 1980s, many of their parent companies were under financial pressure. As corporate America tightened its belt, alternative, less-expensive ways to utilize business aircraft were sought.

Aircraft management companies stepped in to assume the duties of flight departments for companies that wanted to avoid the expense of maintaining in-house aviation staff and facilities. Hundreds of business aircraft were operated under contract by aircraft management firms such as Aviation Methods, Executive Air Fleet, Jet Fleet and PHH, which acquired Beckett Aviation in 1985.

The following year, Executive Jet Aviation (EJA) introduced the concept of fractional ownership. EJA's NetJets program enabled a company to purchase as little as a one-eighth share of an aircraft and have that aircraft (or one similar to it) operated by EJA. Fractional ownership lowered the barriers to involvement in business aviation because the capital costs of owning a fraction of an aircraft were substantially lower than the cost of purchasing an entire aircraft, and a fractional owner could immediately utilize the services of an experienced flight operation.

One of the many technical innovations of D.U. Howard was the TR5000 series thrust reverser for the British Aerospace (Hawker) 800 business jet. This lightweight system was the first all-aluminum thrust reverser.

D.U. Howard

Approximately 100 companies that flew larger aircraft for business were given some relief from restrictive regulations in 1981, when NBAA won an exemption from FAR Part 125. The rule was designed to deal with the questionable operating practices of some commercial operators of retired airline aircraft.

Unfortunately, some longtime business aircraft operators were unable to continue flying during this stormy period. For example, National Distillers and Chemical Corporation, which operated the first Gulfstream II, closed its aviation department after nearly 40 years of business flying.

The ripple effects of such contractions were felt by fixed base operators (FBOs) and aircraft manufacturers alike. A consolidation among aviation support organizations began during this period, and, by 1985, aviation manufacturers started to merge. Formerly independent companies were swallowed up by larger corporations. Beech became part of Raytheon, Piper was obtained by Lear Siegler, Gulfstream Aerospace came under Chrysler's

Main Photo: The Beech Starship incorporates a number of distinctive features, including a forward wing (called a canard), a swept wing with winglets, and two aft-mounted engines.

Inset: The first application of Collins' Pro Line 4 avionics suite was in the Beech Starship.

Business & Commercial Aviation magazine

Collins

King Radio introduced its first digitally tuned navigation/communications radio, the KX 155, in 1980.

wing, General Dynamics bought Cessna, and McDonnell Douglas acquired Hughes Helicopters. In addition, avionics makers joined forces. Bendix and King merged, and Honeywell and Sperry banded together.

Stagnation in new aircraft sales, caused in part by high product liability costs, prompted Cessna to suspend all piston-engine aircraft production in 1986. Nevertheless, most business aviation manufacturers, including Cessna, continued to produce new turbine-powered aircraft and even developed new innovative designs, such as the Beech Starship and Piaggio Avanti.

In the 1980s, crew coordination became increasingly important to the safe operation of new, sophisticated business aircraft. Consequently, many training organizations began offering courses in cockpit resource management (CRM).

detects and plots atmospheric electrical discharges. Also, head-up displays (HUDs), which had been used in military aircraft for some time, were adapted for business aircraft. In 1983, a Canadair Challenger operated by Pentastar Aviation became one of the first business aircraft to receive a HUD made by Flight Dynamics. Development of the first practical collision avoidance systems, known as "threat alert and collision avoidance systems" or "traffic alert collision avoidance systems" (TCAS), began during this era.

The most dramatic change in aircraft cockpits, however, was the

Passing the Baton

In May 1986, NBAA Chairman Preston S. Parish convened a special meeting of the Association's Board of Directors to announce that a search committee had a nominee to replace retiring NBAA President John H. Winant. The choice was Jonathan Howe. The Board concurred, and Howe took the reins on December 1, 1986.

Howe, a 48-year-old attorney, had impressive credentials. He had learned to fly while earning his bachelor's and law degrees at Yale. In 23 years with the FAA, Howe had served in a variety of positions, and by the early 1980s he was director of the agency's Southern Region. He also had an air transport pilot certificate and regularly flew King Airs.

While Howe's aggressive style contrasted with the more reserved demeanor of Winant, many believed that forceful leadership was what was needed to meet the challenges facing NBAA. Howe moved quickly to reorganize NBAA's Washington Staff, putting greater emphasis on government affairs and developing a positive public image for business aviation.

The first major crisis to confront Howe was a plan by the Massachusetts Port Authority to institute new fees that would have discouraged business aircraft operations at Boston's Logan Airport. After discussions with Massachusetts officials failed to yield a compromise, NBAA lodged a complaint with the U.S. Department of Transportation (DOT), followed by a lawsuit that asserted that the charges were discriminatory and illegal. The DOT eventually upheld the validity of the complaint, but a federal judge ruled in favor of the airport authority.

In the face of considerable opposition by other parties in the suit, Howe urged an appeal. The appeal was finally

Jonathan Howe (right) succeeded John H. Winant (left) as President of NBAA in 1986. The two were reunited, along with Winant's wife Katie (center), during a ceremony in which a plaque was installed in NBAA's board room to commemorate Winant's 15 years as head of the Association.

made, and the resulting decision in NBAA's favor not only ensured access to Logan but has discouraged other airports from instituting similar discriminatory restrictions. Howe believed that the vigorous response to proposed restrictions at Logan, as well as the opportunity to make the case for business aviation, made the costly effort doubly worthwhile.

The other major victory during Howe's NBAA tenure was gaining an exemption from the most stringent international noise standards for existing aircraft weighing less than 75,000 pounds, which at the time included virtually all business aircraft.

After leaving NBAA in 1991, Howe joined a Washington law firm. In 1997 he became Director General of the Airports Council International in Geneva, Switzerland.

Business & Commercial Aviation magazine

Top: The Aero Commander has proven to be one of the most versatile designs in business aviation. During the late 1970s, Rockwell produced the Model 690B, a turboprop version of Ted Smith's original piston twin.

introduction of electronic flight instrument systems (EFIS), which use cathode ray tubes (CRTs) instead of mechanical gauges to display flight information. The first EFIS was manufactured by Collins and installed in a United Airlines Boeing 767 in 1982. Within a few years, Bendix, Smiths Industries and Sperry, as well as Collins, were offering EFIS units for business aircraft. Soon, EFIS and other electronic cockpit systems and sensors would be linked together. In December 1984, a British Aerospace 800 oper-

Helicopters, such as this Hughes 500, are not just used to transport executives. Many companies utilize rotorcraft to perform utility missions, such as pipeline patrol.

Flying magazine

ated by Turbine Air Management became the first business jet to have an all-digital integrated avionics system.

Software technology was key to the integration of onboard avionics, as well as to the development of a variety of aviation computer services (avcomps) for aircraft maintenance scheduling and recordkeeping, crew scheduling and other flight department management duties. Personal computers were even used to file flight plans with the FAA under the agency's Direct User Access Terminal (DUAT) program.

Computers also were the driving force behind the rapid improvement in flight simulators, especially the realism and detail of their visual displays. The FAA recognized that the dramatic improvement in simulation would permit most, if not all, flight training to be performed on the ground. In 1984, a Dallas-based company called SimuFlite began training business aircraft personnel, entering the arena of simulator-based business aviation training that had been pioneered and served almost exclusively by FlightSafety International, although American Airlines provided training for Citation operators. Later that year Don Nolen, a Learjet 35 pilot for Million Air in Addison, Texas, became the first aviator to earn a type rating by completing all of his flying requirements in a simulator.

Besides using more state-of-the-art simulators for instruction, FlightSafety International, SimuFlite and other training organizations developed new courses in advanced concepts such as cockpit resource management (CRM), which taught pilots how to best coordinate their efforts to fly an aircraft.

NBAA also became directly involved in education. In the late 1970s, the Association launched a series of operations manual workshops, which initially were conducted by NBAA Vice President John A. Pope and aviation insurance expert Robert E. Breiling. In 1984, NBAA and *Business & Commercial Aviation* magazine teamed up to offer seminars on various business aviation topics. Two years later, NBAA and the Colgate Darden Graduate Business School at the University of Virginia presented their first joint seminar titled "Managing the Corporate Aviation Function." The course was to be part of a comprehensive program of graduate level studies

The Upjohn Company's Preston S. Parish (left) succeeded Lee L. Robbins (right) of Corning Glass as Chairman of NBAA in 1985.

Mergers were a hallmark of the 1980s, both among business aircraft operators and manufacturers. During this era, Chrysler acquired Gulfstream Aerospace, and both Chrysler's chief executive Lee Iacocca (left) and Gulfstream CEO Allen E. Paulson (right) attended the 1985 NBAA Convention.

in business aviation management, and in 1987 NBAA set up an educational foundation to coordinate those activities.

The 1980s also saw the advancement of navigation technologies. The first public-use microwave landing system (MLS) was commissioned for instrument approaches at Alaska's Valdez Airport in 1982. Beginning the same year, Loran C navigation equipment specially designed for use in aircraft was offered by companies such as Offshore Navigation and Texas Instruments. These Loran units used signals from a chain of ground-based U.S. Coast Guard stations to establish accurate aircraft position. By the mid-1980s, avionics manufacturers also were building Global Positioning System (GPS) receivers so that civil aircraft operators could use the U.S. military's highly precise NavStar satellite system for navigation.

Precise long-range navigation systems, including such established technologies as inertial navigation and VLF/Omega, as well as the new

The Independent J. Lynn Helms

the aircraft industry and had gained wide recognition for putting Piper Aircraft Corporation back on course.

Helms agreed to take the FAA job with the understanding that he would run the agency his way and without any political considerations. He began implementing his style from day one, arriving for work at 7 and leaving at 5:30.

"I had heard about the 9-to-5 bureaucrats," said Helms, "but after I began coming in early and leaving late, I found the senior people followed my example. I also got approval to install my team and ended up with the greatest bunch you could imagine," he added.

"We were just beginning to percolate when we faced the air traffic controllers strike," recalled Helms. "We knew it was going to happen and we were prepared. We told the truth about not rehiring the strikers, and [President] Reagan backed us."

"We went on from there and got [the ATC system] back on track," said Helms. "I always knew we would need strategic planning to make sense of what was going on, and we finally put together the National Aviation System Plan. Some of it was successful and some was not, but we had made a start."

When J. Lynn Helms was named to head the FAA in 1980, many in business aviation breathed a sigh of relief. For the first time in years, the Administrator would be a person familiar with general aviation. Helms was an executive in

Bombardier

GPS, would prove to be especially important to business aircraft operators flying internationally. U.S. companies had been flying their own aircraft to Europe and the Middle East regularly since the Gulfstream and JetStar entered the fleet in the 1960s. In fact, U.S. Steel made a westbound round-the-world flight in a Grumman Gulfstream in 1962. However, the longer legs of new, more-capable aircraft—particularly "heavy iron" intercontinental jets such as the Gulfstream III, Falcon 50 and Canadair Challenger—made international flying even easier.

Originally, business aircraft operators flying overseas had to rely on international airlines, such as Pan Am or TWA, to provide flight planning assistance, weather forecasting, ATC and overflight clearances and communications services. However, by the early 1980s a group of independent companies, most based in the Houston area, offered complete dispatch services for business aircraft flying abroad, including two-way communications with the home office, 24-hour flight following, continuously updated weather information, flight plans, diplomatic and ATC clearances, ground handling arrangements and fuel credit at locations that routinely required cash. The pioneer in the international handling field was Universal Weather, which started in 1960, and its success spawned Air Routing, Baseops International and other companies.

By the late 1970s, several long-range business jets had emerged, including the wide-body Canadair Challenger.

Another boon to international flying was the advent of Aeronautical Radio Incorporated's (ARINC) Communication Addressing and Reporting System (ACARS), which uses a data link, instead of voice transmissions, to automatically transmit vital flight information from an aircraft to its home base via a VHF network.

As the years went by, business aircraft operators in other nations organized associations similar to NBAA to promote and protect their interests. In 1961, groups were formed in Canada and the United Kingdom. By 1977, a regional organization, the European Business Aviation Association, was created. In 1981, the U.S., British, Canadian, German and European groups formed the International Business Aviation Council (IBAC), which aimed to elevate business aviation's profile worldwide and sought and won official standing with the International Civil Aviation Organization (ICAO).

As Europe moved toward economic union, the aviation regulatory bodies in various countries on the continent began developing Joint Airworthiness Regulations (JARs). IBAC, its members and the General Aviation Manufacturers Association (GAMA) would work for years with the Europeans

Flying to international destinations such as Paris' Le Bourget Airport increased during the 1980s, thanks in part to the longer-range capability of new business jets.

©1997 Mike Vines

to ensure that the JARs would be harmonized with existing and proposed Federal Aviation Regulations (FARs) regarding aircraft certification.

Back home, new regulations—ranging from FAA rules on use of alcohol and drugs to efforts by the Internal Revenue Service (IRS) to tax certain types of business aircraft use—were gnawing at operators. The IRS taxed personal use of a company aircraft, even use of an otherwise empty seat on an aircraft engaged on a legitimate business trip. Another levy imposed a 10-percent luxury tax on sales of new turbine-powered business aircraft, unless the owner could demonstrate that his aircraft was used predominantly for business purposes.

By 1987 confidence in the U.S. air transportation system was low. Airline deregulation was being blamed for poor service and delays, and reports of near-midair collisions rose. The FAA and NTSB publicly disagreed on how best to remedy the situation, making the public question whether it was safe to fly. The law that provided funding for airport and airways improvements was about to expire, and aircraft operators wondered where their trust fund dollars had gone. As air traffic delays increased, so

The spacious cabin of the twin-turbine Sikorsky S-76 made it one of the most popular helicopters among business aircraft operators.

NBAA

In the early 1980s Piper developed a new, high-performance, pressurized, single-engine airplane called the Malibu.

did the rhetoric about re-regulation of the airline industry and imposition of constraints on general aviation flying.

It was in this volatile climate that a change in NBAA leadership occurred in 1986. John H. Winant retired after 29 years with the Association, the first 14 as a Board Member and the last 15 as President. He was succeeded by Jonathan Howe, an attorney and former Director of FAA's Southern Region.

In his first speech as NBAA President designate, Howe said the three great challenges facing business aviation were lack of system capacity, underfunding of airspace and airways improvements and business aviation's poor public image. Soon, NBAA would launch aggressive programs to address those and other problems facing business aviation.

In spite of the momentous changes that occurred in business aviation as a result of new taxes, airline deregulation, noise legislation and media reaction to abuse by a very few but highly visible corporate raiders, business flying grew during the decade. However, the rate of growth slowed substantially, and the number of flight departments began to decrease after reaching a high in 1987. That shrinkage would continue until mid-1991.

Benevolent Business Aviation

Business aviation isn't all business. Aircraft operators pitch in when their neighbors need a helping hand. Two programs that epitomize this spirit are Cessna's Special Olympics Airlift and the Corporate Angel Network.

Cessna CEO Russell W. Meyer, Jr. conceived the idea of using Citation business jets to transport athletes with disabilities to the Special Olympics, and Marilyn Richwine, Meyer's former secretary, has been responsible for making the world's largest peacetime airlift happen.

Because state Special Olympics organizations have limited travel budgets, many athletes with disabilities would not be able to attend the World Games if it were not for the generosity of dozens of Citation operators. Since 1987, these companies have been flying small groups of young people from all across the country to and from the Games. Volunteers help schedule and support the aircraft and supervise the boarding and deplaning of nearly 1,000 people with disabilities in a single day.

While the Special Olympics Airlift occurs once every couple of years, on any given day, the odds are that at least one business aircraft is carrying a cancer patient, thanks to the Corporate Angel Network (CAN), a volunteer organization that arranges for patients to use empty seats on company aircraft to travel to treatment centers across the United States.

CAN, which is headquartered at Westchester County Airport in White Plains, New York, was the brainchild of Priscilla H. "Pat" Blum, a local pilot and recovering cancer patient who believed that if ambulatory cancer patients could hitch a ride on business aircraft to get to specialized treatment centers, they could increase their chances of survival. She reasoned that such transportation would not cost either the patient or participating company any money because only regularly scheduled business flights would be used. Furthermore, use of otherwise empty seats would mean no additional insurance or tax liability for companies but would generate favorable publicity.

Working with Jay Weinberg, another recovering cancer patient, Blum arranged CAN's first flight. On December 22, 1981, a King Air operated by Safe Flight Instrument Corporation and flown by its founder, Dr. Leonard Greene, carried Michael Burnett, a 19-year-old patient at Memorial Sloan Kettering Hospital in New York City, from White Plains to Detroit so he could be home for Christmas. Since then about 500 companies have made thousands of flights on behalf of CAN.

Corporate Angel Network founders Priscilla "Pat" Blum and Jay Weinberg.

©1997 Marianne Barcellona

Through the generosity of business aircraft operators, almost 200 Cessna Citation business jets transported nearly 1,500 athletes free of charge to the Special Olympics in St. Paul, Minnesota in 1991.

Cessna

CHAPTER 7

Present-Day Business Aviation

A development of the Jet Commander, the Israeli-built Westwind II was one of the first business jets to feature winglets, which were mounted on top of the aircraft's tip tanks.

©1997 Paul Bowen

By the early 1990s, the generation that had helped business aviation take off during the early 1950s was fading away. Most of the World War II veterans who had piloted Beech 18s, Douglas DC-3s and converted military transports had retired. Aircraft company founders Dwane Wallace and Olive Ann Beech, as well as marketing gurus Leddy Greever and Charles "Chuck" Vogeley, passed on. But bright, well-trained business aviation professionals stepped in to tackle the new challenges facing the community.

What they inherited was an industry that was poised to grow but was being constrained by a variety of economic, political and operational factors. A new era of fiscal conservatism followed the stock market crash of 1987, making businesses wary of investing in new capital equipment, such as business aircraft.

In addition, many companies cut back their travel schedules following the outbreak of the Gulf War in 1991. Uncertainties over the price and availability of fuel, as well as the threat of terrorism, were major factors. Tightened airport security rules, aimed at protecting airline passengers, also hampered business aircraft operations. Member companies of the General Aviation Manufacturers Association (GAMA) shipped fewer new aircraft in 1991 than in any year since the end of World War II, delivering a total of just over 1,000 aircraft.

As it would turn out, 1991 was business aviation's nadir. The reduction in flight departments that began in the mid-to-late 1980s continued as corporate consolidation, staff downsizing and eventually the recession of the early 1990s took their toll. Between 1987 and the end of 1991, the number

Cessna

of flight departments operating turbine aircraft fell by about 10 percent. But in the early 1990s, business aviation emerged with a new and profoundly different importance, slowly at first, but with a growing momentum.

As "rightsized" companies struggled to increase the productivity of the managers who remained, the need to travel more efficiently grew, consequently so did the need for business aviation. The "communications revolution" had not replaced the need to travel. Quite to the contrary, fax machines, cellular phones and e-mail had simply quickened the pace of business and increased the need to be face-to-face with customers and business partners before the competition arrived to seize the increasing number of opportunities for market expansion as the economy edged toward recovery. Time was becoming a manager's most precious commodity.

Powerful Allison AE3007C engines make the Citation X, which can cruise at more than 500 knots, one of the fastest civil aircraft flying today.

©1997 Paul Brou

The top-of-the-line Learjet is the Pratt & Whitney-powered Model 60, which can carry as many as 10 passengers or can fly more than 2,000 nautical miles.

Business aviation, with its ability to link company managers with 10 times the number of locations served by the scheduled airlines and 100 times the locations served with timely commercial arrivals and departures, took on an increasingly important role. Managers were able to hold company confidential conversations on board business aircraft without fear that a stranger would be listening. Travel time became productive time. This form of business transportation was gaining broader acceptance as a vital part of a company's communication process.

Flight departments transitioned from isolated islands with little connection to the normal corporate structure to integral parts of the support staff. Consequently, the need for management training among flight department managers grew, and all of business aviation became more sophisticated.

126

Business Aviation's Leading Advocate

NBAA President John W. "Jack" Olcott is arguably business aviation's biggest fan. A pilot with more than 7,500 hours of flight time in everything from gliders to business jets, there is no one who believes more fervently in the importance of business flying to the economy and the nation as a whole.

In the few short years he has been with NBAA, he has focused the Association's energies on demonstrating and proclaiming the value of business aviation. Two prominent examples of those efforts are the "No Plane, No Gain" public advocacy program (conducted in cooperation with the General Aviation Manufacturers Association) and NBAA's Travel$ense software, which helps companies quantify and document how flying on a company aircraft is cost-effective.

Before he came to NBAA in 1992, Olcott was spreading the word about business aviation as a Vice President and Group Publisher with McGraw Hill, where he was in charge of a number of publications, including *Business & Commercial Aviation* magazine. Earlier he was a Senior Editor with *Flying* magazine.

Olcott earned bachelor's and master's degrees in aeronautical engineering from Princeton University and an MBA from Rutgers. He began his aviation career in 1962 at Linden Flight Service in New Jersey, and he participated in a number of private and government flight research programs, including one that took him to India.

Throughout his career, Olcott has been involved in a host of aviation research and educational efforts. He has won numerous awards for his contributions to FAA, NASA and industry advisory committees. Perhaps most impressive, he practices what he preaches about business aviation by flying a Beech Baron.

©1997 Paul Brou

Even before becoming NBAA President in 1992, John W. Olcott was a staunch advocate of business aviation.

While the vibrant economy that would dominate the mid-1990s helped the growth of business aviation just as it helped American business in general, recovery of the business aviation community began long before even the most insightful pundits predicted our nation's sustained economic recovery. In many ways, business aviation was the right form of transportation for rightsizing.

Even before air traffic began to climb again, major changes in the ATC system were underway. In 1988, the FAA had completed the transition to a new computer system, as the last of 20 air route traffic control centers (ARTCCs) received the so-called "host computer." The agency also was planning to replace all instrument landing systems (ILS) with microwave landing systems (MLS) by 1998.

However, technical problems with MLS, the growing popularity of Loran C and the emergence of a new, even more-promising technology—satellite navigation (satnav)—caused the FAA to rethink its plans. After considering the possibilities of using the U.S. military's Navstar Global Positioning System (GPS), the FAA announced it would support a multi-phase transition to satellite navigation. By 1995, the International Civil Aviation Organization (ICAO) had cleared the way for worldwide acceptance of satellite navigation by modifying its policy that all international airports be outfitted with MLS.

The transition to GPS navigation moved rapidly and is expected to be complete by 2010, after which all remaining conventional ground-based navigation aids are to be decommissioned. However, NBAA and other general aviation groups have urged continued funding and upgrade of the Loran C network as a backup for GPS through at least 2010.

When fully implemented, GPS is expected to permit "free flight"—a system in which pilots can choose their own routes and altitudes. Theoretically, air traffic controllers would only intervene when traffic conflicts might occur. Many business jets already have realized the benefits of such flexible operating

NBAA

Top: Perhaps best known as the former director of Xerox's flight department, Richard J. Van Gemert has been involved in business aviation for more than three decades.

Bottom: The North American Free Trade Agreement has created new business opportunities for U.S. companies in Mexico. The modern FBO at Los Cabos receives business aircraft that visit the Baja region.

AMR Combs

The Gulfstream G-IVSP is one of business aviation's leading long-range airplanes. The twin-turbofan-powered aircraft can seat up to 19 people or fly more than 4,000 nautical miles.

Gulfstream Aerospace

rules by participating in the FAA's national route program, which allows certain high-altitude, long-range flights within the United States to be conducted in a manner approaching the principles of free flight.

The development of satellite communications (satcom) also has been a boon to business aviation. Since the first business aviation satcom system was commissioned on a Gulfstream IV in November 1990, hundreds of business aircraft have been able to enjoy secure voice, facsimile and data communications through the International Mobile Satellite Organization (INMARSAT) network.

Satnav and satcom proved particularly important to international operators that were flying to exploit newly opened or expanding markets, such as China and the countries of the former Soviet Union. Some aircraft service providers also made it easier to operate overseas through special new programs. Executive Jet Aviation (EJA) started its Netjets Europe fractional ownership program in 1996, and both Bombardier and Dassault Falcon Jet set up business jet charter services in China.

David M. Sheehan managed a diverse fleet of aircraft during his tenure as Director of Aircraft Services for Mobil Oil. He also served as Vice Chairman of NBAA.

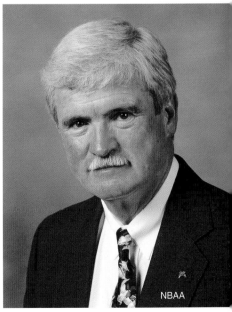

NBAA

Flying outside the United States, however, still wasn't always simple or inexpensive. Some business aircraft operators found out the hard way that temporary registration certificates, so-called "pink slips," are not valid outside the United States. Customs officials, under pressure to be on the lookout for potential drug smugglers, sometimes confiscated the unregis-

Excellence By Design

For more than 50 years, Edward J. Swearingen has not only designed several innovative new aircraft, he has conceived a series of beautifully designed and executed performance-enhancing modifications for existing airplanes. Early on, there was a Twin Beech air stair door and a combustion monitor that was the first exhaust gas temperature gauge. Then there was a nose landing gear steering system for a converted World War II aircraft, which gave Swearingen enough money to start his own aircraft business.

Being an independent businessman had been Swearingen's goal ever since he quit school at age 16 to work as an aircraft mechanic in his home town of San Antonio. He used part of his earnings to take flying lessons and buy an airplane. Then he met another equally resourceful, self-taught aviation innovator—D.U. "Dee" Howard—and they set up their own aircraft repair and overhaul shop.

"Bill Lear stopped by a couple of times and seemed to be impressed with what we were doing," said Swearingen. After Swearingen adapted one of Lear's jet-fighter autopilots for use in a Beech 18, Lear hired him to help modify Lockheed Lodestars into Learstars for business use.

"You can imagine what that was like," recalled Swearingen. "I was 26 years old and working with one of the brightest, most inventive and successful aviation people in the world. The place was a haven for innovative designers and resourceful people."

"I had a magnificent relationship with Lear," said Swearingen, "but after several years I decided it was time to start my own business. I flew back to San Antonio and on February 1, 1959 started The Swearingen Company. My idea was to do whatever jobs I could find and use the money to prepare for my goal: to manufacture aircraft of my own design.

"First I helped Dee Howard modify the Ventura for corporate use. I designed a fully enclosed landing gear door kit for Aero Commander and did a string of design jobs for Piper, including the prototype of the Twin Comanche. Later, I reworked the Lockheed JetStar into the JetStar II."

After completing performance enhancement jobs on the Beech Queen Air and Piper Apache, Swearingen was ready to build his first airplane. The Pratt & Whitney PT6-powered Swearingen Merlin became a popular turboprop business airplane.

Swearingen subsequently modified the design to become the Metro, a regional airliner that Fairchild produced. He spent some time exploring the possibility of a supersonic business jet before turning his attention to designing a highly efficient business jet. The result was the SJ30, the latest version of which should be FAA certificated soon.

Edward J. Swearingen

©1997 Paul Brou

Logan International Airport

tered aircraft of legitimate operators. The FAA solved the problem by telex-ing registrations to aircraft owners.

Business aircraft often had trouble gaining access to major airports in Japan. Canada was one of several countries that turned over administration of their ATC systems to not-for-profit corporations that charge user fees for various handling services. Also, beginning in 1997, business aircraft operators had to meet stringent operational and equipment requirements to fly on pre-ferred routes over the North Atlantic. In fact, the number and scope of changes in international procedures prompted NBAA in 1996 to issue a revised edition of its oceanic flying operations and procedures manual.

Perhaps the greatest threat to international business aviation during this era was European efforts to curtail operation of aircraft that met FAR Part 36 Stage 2 (known as ICAO Chapter 2 internationally) of a three-level, weight-based noise-rating system. In effect, noise restrictions would have been used to reduce air traffic congestion. European authorities planned to ban Stage 2 aircraft operations beginning in 1990. However, NBAA noted that Stage 2 aircraft weighing less than 75,000 pounds actually make less

A major battleground for airport access during the late 1980s was Boston's Logan International Airport. Massport, the operator of New England's largest hub, had sought to establish fees that would have discouraged many business aircraft from using the field.

In today's global economy, business aviation has become international in scope. Magec Aviation is one of the FBOs that supports business flying in Great Britain.

noise than the quietest (Stage 3) airliners, and European authorities subsequently exempted those smaller aircraft from their new regulations.

NBAA had helped set an important precedent, one that was codified in the Airport Noise and Capacity Act of 1990. The U.S. law protected

Israel Aircraft Industries' Astra SPX is one of several business jets that uses an improved version of the AlliedSignal TFE 731 turbofan to fly faster, yet more efficiently. The Astra SPX received FAA certification in January 1996.

Stage 2 aircraft weighing less than 75,000 pounds by requiring federal approval of any local limits regarding operation of those airplanes, which was important since major airports in New York and Los Angeles had been contemplating such restrictions.

The Bell 230 is one of a class of twin-turbine helicopters that have found an important niche in the business aviation fleet.

  The most important battle for airport access, however, would be over the right to operate at Boston's Logan International Airport. In March 1988, the Massport airport authority unveiled its Program for Airport Capacity Efficiency (PACE), which used high fees to discourage use of the airport by smaller aircraft. Within a month, NBAA and other interested parties filed suit in federal court to block the PACE plan but were unsuccessful. However, by the end of the year, the U.S. Department of Transportation (DOT) ruled that PACE was inconsistent with national transportation policy, and in August 1989, an appeals court found that PACE was contrary to federal law. Fees that had been collected at Logan while the PACE plan was in effect during 1988 were refunded.

  While airport access remained one of the major issues for business aircraft operators, they faced other challenges during the early 1990s as well. Crew

Raytheon Aircraft

Top: Contrary to popular belief, most business aircraft, such as this Beech King Air 350, are not used primarily to transport company executives.

Right: Originally developed for use in business jets, electronic flight instrument systems (EFIS) have also been installed in turboprops. This Beech King Air 350 cockpit features the Collins EFIS 86.

Collins

A primary function of NBAA is to maintain a liaison with key government officials. Association President John W. Olcott (second from right) listens as Dan Glickman (left), a former Congressman influential in aviation affairs and later U.S. Secretary of Agriculture, speaks with aircraft industry officials.

pairing and flight and duty times for pilots became important, especially as new longer-range aircraft were developed. Business and commercial aviators also had to deal with the deficiencies of early traffic alert and collision avoidance systems (TCAS), which occasionally gave erroneous conflict-resolution advisories. Once they arrived at an airport, business aircraft operators faced new fees imposed by some fixed base operators (FBOs) that claimed they could no longer afford to offer certain previously complimentary services free of charge.

Raleigh E. Drennon, the retired flight department manager for BFGoodrich, served as NBAA Chairman from 1987 to 1989.

Operators of piston-powered aircraft faced the prospect of having their aircraft engines made obsolete by U.S. Environmental Protection Agency (EPA) regulations banning the use of leaded gasoline. The EPA eventually excluded aviation gasoline and powerplants from those rules. However, operators of underground fuel storage facilities were required to upgrade their tanks and install automatic leak detectors and other devices designed to prevent fuel spills.

After an airline Boeing 737 suffered an inflight structural failure over Hawaii, concerns about the integrity of aging aircraft grew. GAMA responded by developing a continuing airworthiness program for older general aviation airplanes. The use of bogus or unapproved parts by unscrupulous or unsuspecting repair facilities also became an issue, as did the possible susceptibility of

Sophisticated, full-motion flight simulators, such as this Dassault Falcon 2000 unit operated by FlightSafety International, have allowed business aircraft pilots to receive most of their flight training without ever leaving the ground.

electronic aircraft equipment to interference from high-energy radiated fields. Stiffer standards for testing and shielding of avionics resulted.

During this period, by-the-book application of FAA rules had rankled many business aircraft operators, so FAA Administrator James Busey announced a comprehensive review of the agency's general aviation enforcement program. The goal was to reorient agency inspectors to achieve compliance through education, rather than through automatic imposition of fines or suspension of licenses or certificates.

Despite the FAA's ATC modernization efforts, system capacity still trailed demand, which sparked efforts to convert closed military air bases to civilian use. More radical proposals called for privatizing airports and establishing a new government corporation to run the ATC system.

Washington, D.C.'s Dulles International Airport was originally shunned by the airlines. But the field has always been a favorite stop for business aircraft operators.

Many operators demanded an overhaul of the agency itself. Believing that the Department of Transportation (DOT) was exerting undue influence on the FAA, several federal lawmakers proposed legislation to make the agency independent of the DOT. Other congressmen sought to impose a "trigger tax," which would have rolled back aviation taxes if a minimum amount of trust fund money was not spent each year on improving the aviation infrastructure. Personnel and acquisition reforms were implemented at the FAA in 1996, but most business aircraft operators believed that much more needed to be done to make the agency responsive and efficient.

Besides pressing for additional FAA reform during the early 1990s, NBAA intensified its efforts to increase the understanding and acceptance of business aviation among regulators and the general public. The Association's advocacy efforts bore fruit in terms of several victories on tax issues. For example, NBAA won clarification of the affiliated group exemption.

As the reliability of turbine power-plants has increased, single-engine turboprops, such as the TBM 700, have won a following among business aircraft users.

Flying magazine

©1997 Paul Brou

Helicopters remain the quickest way to get downtown in many metropolitan areas, thus making rotorcraft an important segment of the business aviation fleet.

NBAA and other groups also finally convinced lawmakers to repeal the 10-percent luxury tax on new aircraft. Although the tax originally included a provision exempting operators who could demonstrate that the equipment was utilized predominantly for business, many companies were understandably reluctant to have the IRS scrutinize their records.

The industry's greatest victory, however, came when President Bill Clinton signed the General Aviation Revitalization Act of 1993. The product liability reform law, which was supported by manufacturers and operators alike, limited to 18 years the time that a maker of general aviation aircraft or components could be held liable for accidents involving their products.

Enactment of the law sparked a revival in general aviation aircraft manufacturing. Cessna, as promised, made plans to resume production of piston-powered airplanes, and a host of manufacturers rolled out new turbine aircraft. New types of equipment designed for business aviation includ-

138

For many years, Beech marketed business jets built by other manufacturers. But now the renamed company, Raytheon Aircraft, sells several of its own jet designs, including the Beechjet, which is an improved version of the Mitsubishi Diamond II business jet.

Flying magazine

Trained as an engineer, Max E. Bleck was president of each of the "Big Three" general aviation manufacturers—Beech, Cessna and Piper—during his 40-plus-year career.

ed tilt-rotor aircraft, single-engine business jets, helicopters with no tail rotors and ultra-long-range business jets. In addition, regional jets, such as the Canadair RJ, were adapted for business use.

In the 15 years since the zenith of general aviation aircraft production, many of the major players in the manufacturing sector had changed. Raytheon Aircraft acquired the Hawker line of business jets from British Aerospace. Cessna's new parent company was Textron, which had sold its Lycoming turbine engines to AlliedSignal. Canada's Bombardier scooped up de Havilland, Learjet and Shorts. Piper spent four years in Chapter 11 bankruptcy before emerging as a streamlined company. West Germany's BMW and Rolls-Royce of England teamed up to build aircraft engines for the new ultra-long-range business jets. Finally, Bell and Boeing announced plans to collaborate on a new civil tilt-rotor aircraft.

Gulfstream Aerospace studied the possibility of building a supersonic business jet (SSBJ) but decided that such a design was not yet viable.

Worldwide support is important to business aircraft operators, especially NBAA Member Companies, the majority of which fly overseas. Raytheon Aircraft's service center in Chester, England offers complete support for Hawker business jets.

My, How You Have Grown!

Each year the number and variety of business aircraft displayed at the NBAA Convention grows. Although some models are exhibited on the floor of the trade show, most of the more than 150 business aircraft shown are parked at a nearby airport.

©1997 Paul Brou

Development of the NBAA Annual Meeting & Convention into the largest purely civil aviation exhibition in the world is a source of pride not just for the Association, but for the entire business aviation community. Approximately 25,000 people come each year to see the latest business aviation products and services at the NBAA Show.

Of course, the Convention is where much of the important official business of the Association is conducted. It also is where manufacturers and their customers get to exchange information, particularly during the numerous Maintenance & Operations sessions. In addition, seminars and workshops held before, during and after the Show offer educational and networking opportunities for business aircraft operators.

Surprisingly, there was a time when no trade show was held in conjunction with the NBAA Annual Meeting. However, enterprising aviation sales people quickly found ways to connect with their customers using that venue. In the early 1950s, when few formal evening activities were scheduled during the Annual Meeting, AiResearch's Scott E. Miller organized a cocktail party for NBAA Members in his company's hotel suite. Competitors promptly copied the practice, and soon the Association itself was hosting an evening reception.

In the early days, vendors set up tabletop displays and handed out brochures. Later, those exhibits moved into larger, organized rooms within the Convention hotel. By the 1960s, clever manufacturers found ways to squeeze airplanes into exhibit areas. Finally, in 1970 the trade show was held for the first time in a convention hall, Denver's Currigan Center.

For a decade beginning in the mid-1950s, flight demonstrations were conducted during the NBAA Show.

However, they were discontinued because of fears that overly aggressive flying of high-performance aircraft could lead to a mishap. Starting in 1970, the NBAA's single "Airport Day" was replaced by the familiar three-day-long static aircraft display.

As the NBAA Show grew in size and importance, the aviation press began reporting on Convention activities. The *Show Daily* started covering NBAA Meetings in 1960, and *Aviation International News* got its start at the 1972 Show.

Today, the Convention is NBAA's largest single source of revenue. It requires sophisticated marketing and year-round management by the Association's professional Staff, as well as the assistance of a committee of local volunteers in the host city.

©1997 Paul Brou

The NBAA Convention has grown to become the world's largest exhibition dedicated solely to civil aviation equipment and services. Approximately 25,000 people attend the event annually.

Corning uses Dornier 328 twin-turboprop, regional airliners to shuttle personnel between its headquarters in upstate New York and several other company facilities on the East Coast.

Corning

However, Gulfstream and Bombardier each launched an ultra-long-range business jet capable of flying up to 6,500 nautical miles nonstop. They are designated the Gulfstream V and Global Express, respectively.

Innovative developments have not been restricted to airframes. New avionics and equipment—including enhanced ground proximity warning sys-

Left: J. Mac McClellan has been observing business aviation for many years, first as a writer for Business & Commercial Aviation *magazine and later as Editor-in-Chief of* Flying *magazine.*

Right: Noted for his knowledge of aviation electronics, Richard N. Aarons, Editor of Business & Commercial Aviation *magazine, coined the term "avcomps" for aviation computer services.*

©1997 Robert B. Parke

Business & Commercial Aviation magazine

tems, TCAS-I, forward-looking wind shear radar, digital cockpit voice recorders and head-up displays—are helping operators fly safely and efficiently.

The trend in aircraft manufacturing today is toward integration. For
example, multi-sensor navigation systems have begun to replace single-sensor
units in business aircraft, many of which are being outfitted with GPS.
Furthermore, airframe builders are working closely with avionics and engines
manufacturers to tie major systems together in a single package controlled by a
powerful central computer. Such sophisticated equipment promises to take
business aviation to new heights.

The Canadair Challenger 601-3R business jet features an improved version of the General Electric CF34 powerplant.

Bombardier

A new class of airplane that is expected to join the business fleet in the near future is the single-engine jet. A proof-of-concept model of the six-seat VisionAire Vantage has been flying since late 1996, and production versions of the airplane are expected to enter service in 1999.

VisionAire

CHAPTER 8

The Future of Business Aviation

Business & Commercial Aviation magazine

As business aviation prepares to enter the 21st century, it continues to face many of the same challenges that prompted the formation of the Corporation Aircraft Owners Association 50 years ago: lagging airport and airways capacity, a rising regulatory burden, and increasing acquisition and operating costs.

Although Gulfstream Aerospace's proposed supersonic business jet could not overcome the cost and technical challenges of the late 1980s, many believe that an SSBJ eventually will be built.

Airport and airways capacity still has failed to keep pace with the growth of air traffic. Because the number of airline flights, especially to and from developing nations, is expected to grow substantially in the coming years, there will be more competition between air carriers and business aviation for space at larger airports worldwide, especially at busy hub facilities that already have constraints on the number of takeoffs and landings they can handle.

In addition to having to fight for equal access to large airports, business aviation will need to work to save smaller landing fields, especially urban facilities, from developers who would use the land for other purposes. Concerted, coordinated efforts by airport advocates—such as the campaign that saved Chicago's Meigs Field in 1997—will help communities realize the substantial positive local economic impact of general aviation airports and how each airfield is part of a national transportation system that facilitates commerce.

Other components of the crusade to preserve airports will ensure that surrounding land is zoned properly and developed for compatible uses. Also, improving technology and techniques to mitigate aircraft noise, including the retirement of the vast majority of the noisier aircraft by the turn of the century, will help make airports good neighbors to nearby residents.

On the regulatory front, the trend toward establishing one level of commercial aviation safety in the United States, including more stringent standards for pilots, equipment and procedures, will increase the regulatory burden of business aircraft operators. On the other hand, efforts to harmonize U.S. and international aviation operating and certification standards offer opportunities and challenges. Common, sensible international certification standards will make it easier for makers of business aircraft to sell their products worldwide. However, imposition of unnecessarily strict operating rules, such as European regulations governing extended twin-engine operations (ETOPS) over the North Atlantic, could diminish the operational flexibility of business aircraft.

Perhaps the greatest threats to business aviation, however, are recurring government attempts to impose taxes and user fees on the industry. Recent proposals include everything from per-flight fees and itemized charges for use of a variety of air traffic control (ATC) services to levies for certificating aircraft designs. Numerous cost-allocation studies have been performed to determine what it costs the government to provide various support services to aviation. An Administration goal is to establish a fee schedule requiring aviation system users to pay the entire cost of running the Federal Aviation Administration (FAA). But many in the business aviation community contend that such a financing scheme ignores the contribution that aviation makes to national economic activity and development.

Left: Production of the Galaxy intercontinental business jet got underway in early 1997. The Israeli-built twin-engine aircraft is expected to enter service in 1999.

Right: Raytheon's Premier I is the first in a planned series of new business aircraft to feature composite airframes built using advanced techniques that reduce manufacturing costs.

Galaxy Aerospace

Raytheon Aircraft

NBAA and other aviation organizations have argued against transition to an unproven and risky user-fee system, noting that the traditional combination of aviation excise taxes (sales taxes on airline tickets, air cargo shipments and general aviation fuel, which are deposited into an aviation trust fund) and contributions from the federal government's general fund has proven to be an effective, steady, reliable and abundant source of revenue for the FAA. Critics of 100-percent user funding contend that an aviation system supported only by user fees would be undercapitalized and underutilized, cumbersome and expensive to administer, include economic disincen-

The Gulfstream V has launched the era of the ultra-long-range business jet. The aircraft, which has a nonstop range of 6,500 nautical miles, was certificated by the FAA in April 1997.

The Emergence of Fractional Ownership

Many companies overlook the advantages of business aviation simply because of the costs and specialized knowledge needed to start a flight department. Since the late 1980s, however, a segment of business aviation known as fractional ownership has emerged.

Pioneered by Richard Santulli and NetJets, a division of Executive Jet Aviation, fractional ownership enables a company to purchase as little as one-eighth of an aircraft and have that aircraft (or one identical to it) operated by the fractional ownership provider. Fractional ownership has lowered the barriers to involvement in business aviation because the capital costs of owning a fraction of an aircraft are substantially lower than purchasing an entire aircraft and a fractional owner can immediately utilize the services of an experienced flight operation.

Several companies now provide programs in the United States and Europe for fractional owners. The largest is NetJets, followed by Bombardier's Business Jet Solutions, which operates under the name of FlexJets. Raytheon Aircraft also has a fractional ownership program.

Additional programs are expected to be set up in South America, the Middle East and the Asia/Pacific region.

Most companies purchasing fractional ownership shares are new to business aviation, having never owned or operated a business aircraft. Several of those companies, however, have expanded their use of business aviation to the point where they have developed their own flight departments.

While some existing flight departments feel threatened by fractional ownership, surveys of NBAA Member Companies indicate that most aviation department managers look upon fractional ownership as a resource that, properly managed, allows a flight department to provide additional services to satisfy a company's travel needs.

As utilization increases, which it often does when companies have an opportunity to experience the benefits of business aviation, many fractional owners will transition to in-house flight departments, according to NBAA surveys. Thus, fractional ownership is an effective means for bringing the advantages of business aviation to a potentially large market for air transportation.

© 1997 Paul Brou

The Bell XV-15 tilt rotor was the test bed for a new type of aircraft that can take off and land vertically like a helicopter yet has the speed and range of a turboprop airplane. First flight of the new Bell/Boeing 609 tilt-rotor is anticipated in July 1999, and initial deliveries are expected in 2001.

General Electric and Boeing have teamed up to provide a larger-cabin aircraft that can fly nearly as far as the new ultra-long-range business jets. First delivery of the Boeing 737 derivative is slated for the end of 1998.

tives for safe operations and ignore the contribution that aviation makes to the country's economy.

Although the aviation excise taxes were abandoned in 1996, they were temporarily reinstated by Congress in 1997. In the final analysis, the Congress will ultimately have a large say in determining how the U.S. aviation system of the future will be funded.

Regardless of the burdens that business aviation may be asked to shoulder in the coming years, the industry's fortunes in general will continue to be tied to the transportation needs of the companies that operate aircraft. Because business opportunities require prompt and efficient response, U.S. business aviation activity has grown substantially since 1992. In 1996, American general aviation concluded its safest year of flying in a decade and a half, and U.S. general aviation aircraft manufacturers posted record billings.

Another factor contributing to the resurgence of business aviation has been the General Aviation Revitalization Act, a law limiting manufacturers' product liability. Since the legislation was enacted in 1994, Cessna has restarted production of single-engine piston-powered airplanes, and manufacturers have begun to realize the fruits of their investment in research and development during the lean years of the late 1980s and early 1990s. More new general aviation aircraft—including the Cessna Citation Excel, Israel Aircraft

The Boeing Company

148

Industries Galaxy and Raytheon Premier—will be introduced between now and the year 2000 than were unveiled in the entire previous decade. In fact, several new classes of business aircraft are expected to emerge.

The first new type of business aircraft to enter service will be ultra-long-range jets such as the Gulfstream V and Bombardier Global Express. These large, twin-engine business jets are designed to fly eight passengers and a crew of four at least 6,500 nautical miles nonstop, which will allow business aircraft to fly for the first time directly between cities such as New York and Tokyo or London and Singapore.

In addition, Boeing and General Electric are teaming up to provide a corporate version of the 737 airliner that will have a range of 6,000 nautical miles. The long flights made possible by the ultra-long-range jets will require a major shift in the man-machine interface, including close monitoring of crew flight and duty times to prevent fatigue.

The logical follow-on to the new ultra-long-range jets is a supersonic transport that would reduce travel time on longer trips, especially transoceanic flights across the Pacific. Experts are divided about the prospects for a supersonic business aircraft in the near future. While some believe that it is possible to overcome the technical and environmental hurdles of building a relatively small aircraft that could fly faster than the speed

Bombardier claims that its Global Express will have the longest non-stop range of any business jet (6,700 nautical miles at its long-range cruise speed) when it enters service in 1998.

Bombardier

Business & Commercial Aviation magazine

Rockwell Collins

Rockwell Collins' Pro Line 21 avionics suite will be used in several new-generation aircraft, including the new Bell/Boeing 609 tilt-rotor. The system features eight-inch by ten-inch liquid-crystal displays that present flight data in a variety of easy-to-use formats.

of sound, all agree that such an aircraft would be very expensive and would require years more research to perfect. Because business aviation is all about minimizing travel time, perhaps someone will realize Allen Paulson's dream of a supersonic business jet.

Another new class of airplane that is expected to emerge is the single-engine business jet. For example, a proof-of-concept model of the six-seat Visionaire Vantage has been flying since late 1996. Production versions of the airplane are expected to enter service in 1999. While single-engine turboprops have been around for several years, many of these aircraft are used in utility roles. Therefore, it remains to be seen whether the traditionally conservative business aircraft operators will embrace single-engine jets, despite the fact that the inflight shut down rate of modern turbofan powerplants is extremely low.

An even more radical aircraft that will be offered for business use is the Bell/Boeing Model 609 tilt-rotor. This six- to nine-passenger, twin-engine aircraft can take off and land vertically like a helicopter yet has the speed and range of a turboprop airplane. The pressurized $10 million aircraft, with an operational ceiling of 25,000 feet, is to be certificated for instrument flight and operations in known icing conditions and will have an advanced glass cockpit and fly-by-wire flight controls. First flight is anticipated in July 1999, and initial deliveries are expected in 2001.

Tilt-rotor aircraft are expected to be especially useful in city-center to city-center transportation because they would be able to use existing heliports. Thus, total trip time would be reduced, compared to flying a fixed-wing aircraft to an airport and then using ground vehicles for transportation to a final destination. However, critics say that civil tilt-rotor aircraft, like corporate helicopters, will only enjoy limited success because of the scarcity of downtown heliports and the higher expense of operating and maintaining rotary-wing aircraft, compared with fixed-wing machines. A tilt-rotor, however, is expected to have a cost per mile about one-half that of helicopters.

Makers of conventional aircraft are expanding use of composite materials and applying new cost-reducing manufacturing techniques to airframe designs. For example, the computer-designed and manufactured

Allen E. Paulson: There Will Be an SSBJ!

"You bet I've still got my eye on the supersonic business jet (SSBJ)," said Allen E. Paulson, chairman emeritus of Gulfstream Aerospace Corporation, who believes it will be the next major step for corporate aviation.

"I believe we can beat the sonic boom and come up with an airplane about the same size as the Gulfstream V that will have about a 4,500-nautical-mile range. We've been talking to Lockheed's Skunk Works as well as Pratt & Whitney and General Electric. There is a lot of new technology out there. It will be a while yet, but it will happen."

Paulson started out as an airplane mechanic for TWA in the 1940s and served in the U.S. Army Air Corps during World War II. After the war, he returned to TWA as a flight engineer, learned to fly under the G.I. bill and soon went into business for himself, launching several companies devoted to aircraft modification, maintenance and design.

In the mid-1970s, Grumman, maker of the pioneering Gulfstream I business airplane, decided to spin off its corporate aviation division in order to concentrate on its military business. Paulson saw an opportunity and with a partner bought the company. It didn't take long before the independent-minded Paulson knew he had to be the boss. He suggested to his partner that they flip a coin for ownership of the company, with the winner buying out the loser. Paulson won.

Paulson quickly focused his energies on making Gulfstream aircraft world leaders. The Gulfstream II, III and IV twinjets followed the twin-turboprop Gulfstream I, each setting a new standard for long-range business jets. In recent years Paulson has set round-the-world speed records in his Gulfstream IV.

Paulson is scheduled to become the proud owner of the first certificated Gulfstream V. A quiet and modest man, he has been showered with degrees, awards and honors (including NBAA's prestigious Meritorious Service Award for lifetime contributions to aviation) and has just about everything he could want, including his own golf course. And one of these days he expects to be the proud owner of the first supersonic business jet.

Gulfstream Aerospace

composite airframe of the Raytheon Premier business jet has fewer parts than an aluminum aircraft, and those parts are more precisely manufactured yet less costly to produce. Not only do these airframe elements have fewer imperfections and fit together better, their inherent strength means that the structure need not be as thick. The result is a fuselage diameter that has a larger interior dimension compared to metal aircraft.

Application of computer technology and miniaturized electronics is allowing avionics to become progressively smaller, lighter, more powerful and reliable. In addition, various functions of cockpit systems are being combined and simplified to reduce pilot workload. Some of the newest electronic equipment that is expected to see wide application in the business aircraft fleet include head-up displays and enhanced ground proximity warning systems.

Progress in powerplants is expected to be evolutionary rather than revolutionary. Use of new high-temperature materials and lightweight computerized system controls will yield more fuel efficiency and make engines easier to maintain through use of digital downlink of data that will permit

Head-up displays have been used for years in military aircraft to enhance situational awareness in all phases of flight. In the future, an increasing number of business jets will be fitted with units such as this Honeywell/GEC-Marconi HUD 2020, which is installed in a Gulfstream IV.

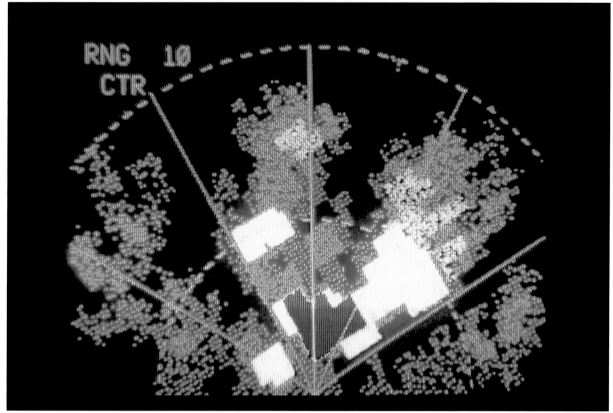

AlliedSignal's enhanced ground proximity warning system paints terrain in much the same way a radar depicts severe weather—in shades of green, yellow and red. A solid red area, which signifies the greatest threat, is displayed when an aircraft is 30 seconds from a projected ground impact.

better trend monitoring and diagnosis of malfunctions and anomalies by ground personnel even before an aircraft finishes a flight.

Computer technology also will play an important part in the development of a more efficient ATC system. Ground-based traffic management facilities are being retrofitted with new computers in a sweeping and long-overdue overhaul of the ATC system. New data-link technology will allow transmission of flight-critical information directly between aircraft cockpits and ground-based facilities. By the middle of the next decade, the U.S. ATC system will rely primarily on a network of satellites rather than thousands of ground stations. This will permit aircraft operators to choose the most efficient routes (so-called "free flight") and will allow continuous and automatic aircraft position reporting, even over oceans.

While these technological advances will facilitate the handling of more air traffic, an ongoing challenge for business aviation will be to maintain and improve the industry's excellent safety record. Greater use of flight simulators, including non-motion flight training devices and programs developed for desktop computers, will be an important facet of such safety efforts.

Flight departments already are utilizing computer technology to better manage their business aircraft. Enhanced versions of maintenance as well as management software, such as NBAA's Travel$ense, promise to make the task easier. Also, the collection and distribution of vital aircraft operating information—such as navigation, weather and cost data—to the flight department office or even directly to the aircraft cockpit or cabin via the Internet and datalinks will allow operators to make informed decisions based on real-time information. Managers are expected to use this vast array of information to define, monitor and justify the costs of aircraft operation with increasing precision.

Part of the drive toward better utilization of business aircraft has given rise to the concept of fractional ownership. Such plans allow a company to purchase a portion of a business aircraft, usually a one-eighth or one-quarter share, and for a monthly fee and a flat hourly rate that covers all expenses, guarantee use of an airplane (with several hours notice) for a fixed number of hours each year.

The fractional ownership concept, which was pioneered in the mid-1980s by Executive Jet Aviation, continues to grow in popularity because it often costs companies with low aircraft utilization rates less money than required to obtain and operate their own aircraft. Numerous providers, including several aircraft manufacturers, now offer fractional ownership

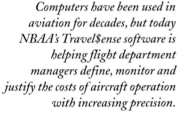

Computers have been used in aviation for decades, but today NBAA's Travel$ense software is helping flight department managers define, monitor and justify the costs of aircraft operation with increasing precision.

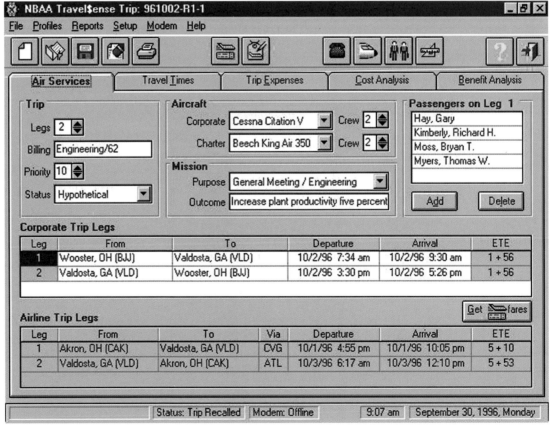

Mal Gormley

plans in the United States and Europe. The vast majority of the participants are companies that have never before owned business aircraft. In some cases, companies that already own airplanes use fractional ownership plans to augment their fleet. Seldom do established aircraft operators sell their aircraft in order to participate.

Although the worldwide market for fractional ownership has been estimated at 150,000 companies, most corporations will continue to own and operate their own aircraft for a variety of reasons. First and foremost, they prefer to have total control over their aircraft in order to maximize efficiency, safety and security. As aircraft utilization increases, an in-house flight department is more cost-effective.

The Gulfstream V ultra-long-range business jet is outfitted with Honeywell's SPZ-8500 integrated avionics system. Flight and systems information is displayed on six eight-inch by eight-inch displays.

Honeywell

The McDonnell Douglas MD 600N is among the newest helicopters. Unlike most other rotorcraft, the aircraft has no tail rotor, which enhances operational safety.

Flight department management styles, reflecting overall trends in corporate cultures, are expected to become more participative and less hierarchical. Pilots and maintenance technicians will be asked to take on more collateral duties in order to boost efficiency and will be rewarded with formal management training that will broaden their career opportunities, both inside and outside the flight department. These people will more likely be college educated, and an increasing number of flight department managers will be selected for their management expertise rather than for their experience as a pilot or mechanic.

One concern is whether there will be an adequate supply of qualified people to fill these management positions in flight departments. While NBAA and colleges offer advanced aviation-management training, airlines and business aircraft operators will compete for the services of a finite pool of qualified pilots, technicians and other support personnel.

A national initiative to attract new people to general aviation was launched in 1997 by GA Team 2000, a non-profit organization. The goal of the program—which is supported by more than 100 aviation companies and groups, including NBAA as a founding member and major contributor—is to attract and train 100,000 new pilots annually by the turn of the century. GA Team 2000 also hopes to highlight and enhance the public's awareness of the value of general aviation.

As aviation enters its second century and the new millennium, the business aviation community is prepared to contribute its unique transportation capabilities to a rapidly changing world. The global economy means that companies will need to be in constant contact with partners and customers worldwide. The advent of new sophisticated communication technologies, such as video conferencing, will make the task easier but will not replace the need for people to conduct business in person. Rather than replacing the need to travel, the communications revolution will quicken the pace of business and increase the need for face-to-face contact.

Time still is money, so the need for fast, on-demand air transportation endures. Despite all the restrictions that may be placed on business aviation, it will always be the fastest and most productive way to get there. And because most companies need to have complete control over their transportation resources in order to maximize efficiency, safety and security, the flight department will continue to be an integral part of the successful and efficient company of the 21st century.

NBAA will remain the champion and guardian of business aviation, fighting unnecessary regulation and restrictions that would diminish the utility of business aircraft while providing daily operational support to operators and promoting business aviation as the ultimate business tool.

First flight of Raytheon's new eight-passenger business jet, the twin Pratt & Whitney PW308A-powered Hawker Horizon, is scheduled to take place in 1999.

Raytheon Aircraft

INDEX

Index

Index

Index

Index

Index